Improving Inventory Record Accuracy

Improving Inventory Record Accuracy

Getting your stock information right

Tony Wild

ELSEVIER
BUTTERWORTH
HEINEMANN

AMSTERDAM BOSTON HEIDELBERG LONDON NEW YORK
OXFORD PARIS SAN DIEGO SAN FRANCISCO SINGAPORE
SYDNEY TOKYO

Elsevier Butterworth-Heinemann
Linacre House, Jordan Hill, Oxford OX2 8DP
200 Wheeler Road, Burlington, MA 01803

First published 2004

British Library Cataloguing in Publication Data
A catalogue record for this book is available from the British Library

Library of Congress Cataloging in Publication Data
A catalog record for this book is available from the Library of Congress

ISBN 0 7506 5900 9

For information on all Butterworth-Heinemann publications visit
our website at www.bh.com

Typeset by Charon Tec Pvt. Ltd, Chennai, India
Printed and bound in Great Britain

Contents

Introduction   1

1 The importance of record accuracy   **4**
Why have accurate records?   4
What accuracy do we need?   5
Identifying the objectives   6
How to measure accuracy   8
Accuracy targets   11
Record pro formas   14

2 Benefits from accurate records   **16**
Effects of record accuracy   16
Counting the cost of inaccuracy   17
Excess inventory   21
Shortages   23

3 Causes of inaccurate records   **25**
Observations of inaccuracy   25
Detailed causes of inaccuracy   28
Analysis of underlying reasons for inaccuracy   28

4 Structures to avoid inaccuracy   **36**
Low inventory levels   36
Zero inventory   37
Vendor-managed inventory   42

Consignment stocks   44
External storage   44

5 Responsibilities for accuracy   46
The foundations of accurate records   46
Information quality   48
Ownership of stock   49
Whose records are they?   50
Locked stores   52
The people factor   54
The recording system   55
Item identity   57
Check digit systems   59

6 The right environment   61
Failsafing (*Pokeyoka*)   61
Flow of material   63
Coordinated batches   63
Control areas   64
Security   65
Stores layout   69
The need for real-time recording   71

7 Batch control   75
Identifying a batch   75
Batch quantities   75
Batch progress control   77

8 Controlling stock movement   84
Simplification   84
Kit marshalling   84
Backflushing   86
Input/output monitoring   88
Company material balance   90
Financial control of stock value   92

9 Inventory checking   93
Inventory counting   93
Inventory checking (stocktaking)   96
Principles of cycle counting   100
ABC analysis   101

Organizing the cycle count 104
Defining the requirements 106

10 Accuracy through information technology 108
Overview 108
Stores computing 108
Bar coding 110
Pitfalls in using bar codes 114
Weigh counting 116
Monitoring manufacturing work in progress by automatic
recording devices 117
Portable terminals 118
Summary of current technological solutions 119
Radio frequency identification 120

11 Record accuracy as a project 122
Project teams 122
Setting up the project 124
Steps for improving record accuracy 125

12 The management of record accuracy 128
Monitoring accuracy 128
Making it happen 129

Appendix 1: Formula for generating stores location check digits 130

Index 133

Introduction

Executives normally expect that people at the sharp end know what they are doing. Of course, they do – well, almost. However, in inventory control there could be items where the records don't agree exactly with the real quantities held in the business; alternatively, sometimes the quantity is correct – it is just finding where the items are located that is the problem. Life at the sharp end is usually a mixture of operating the system and reacting to situations. Often there is great pressure to achieve customer service, delivery on time, response to queries, meetings etc., which results in the 'quick fix' rather than solving the problem. This is especially true for inventory records.

In reality it is much easier to ensure that procedures work properly in the first place. However, people are used to chasing round fixing the immediate problems, and often never get nearer to eliminating the sources of the discrepancies. It takes a little longer now and needs some thought, so the problem remains.

Everyone involved with inventory has a potential issue with data accuracy. The reader who picks up this book is not looking for literary delight, but for ways of fixing some records. It is a practical step on the way to solving a potentially damaging situation – and it is only when it improves that people realize how damaging it really was.

The first step in making data more accurate is to believe that it is possible. That means admitting that there are better ways of doing things. This book is intended to support readers who are looking for ways to change the basic records processes. This does not mean spending a lot of money; it is more a question of time, effort and application. It is a case of using the techniques outlined to ensure that records don't go wrong – a case of 'Mony a mickle maks a muckle', as the Scots would say.

In some cases the methods will be directly usable to improve accuracy; in other cases the basic idea requires putting into the context of the particular inventory in question. In fact, many of the techniques discussed are directly applicable to any type of data.

Record accuracy has become the focus of attention for many businesses because customers are more demanding, expecting the right item to be delivered on time, and competitive pressures don't allow that extra bit of stockholding. Businesses have been offered the opportunity to become much more effective, as long as they are allowed

- the correct information
- the development of better communication and
- integration of systems,

but often organizations fail on the first point.

At the same time, inventory management is under pressure (in most companies) to become more efficient by giving better availability and holding less inventory – and any inventory inaccuracy has a direct effect on these two key performance measures, not to mention long-term survival.

The accuracy of the information is an aspect that has therefore gradually been increasing in importance. The systems only work if the data is correct! Otherwise people are making decisions based on the wrong situations, or mistrusting the data entirely and 'doing their own thing'. With integrated data, there are wide-ranging repercussions.

Where there is a large amount of data there is the opportunity for many errors, some of them major. Usually this is the case with inventory, since many items, large varieties of different items, and fast-changing inventory are involved. The challenge is to measure how much there is – especially where inventory changes rapidly in businesses like consumer retailing and manufacturing processes. With large warehouses there is also the risk of inaccurate recording so that items are missing or not in the right place.

The ways to improve record accuracy are the core subject of this book. The author has amassed some techniques, tried them out in practice, and presents them in a practical style, so that those with the responsibility for record accuracy can use them easily. This is not quantum physics: many of the concepts are very simple, but have to be used in the right way. Everyone will be using some of the techniques. The full benefits result from applying the right combination of the techniques described.

This handbook starts by discussing how to quantify the problem and set sensible targets for improvement. It then focuses on how to make the case for doing something to improve accuracy, which leads on to the financial case for accuracy improvement. By this point the reader should have enough ammunition to go to colleagues who are disinterested and prove to them that something must be done to change – there are graphs to prove how bad it is, and there is information to show the real reduction it causes on operating efficiency and on profits.

OK, do something! The next logical step is to discuss why inventory records do go wrong (this is not really a difficult task!) and then to identify what the major causes are likely to be for the particular inventory in question. What will be more challenging is rectifying the major causes of error.

The remainder of the book illustrates the techniques with which anyone can make their records very accurate. Although errors will never be eliminated by more counting, there is a chapter devoted to inventory counting and perpetual inventory checking for those who need to develop these techniques, and as a basis for normal data maintenance. The secret of success is simplification, responsibility, organization, and using a combination of the other detailed approaches discussed. For those readers who want to get down to it in a logical manner, Chapter 11 outlines the way to run accuracy improvement as a project.

> *This is a practical handbook to solve a practical problem.*

It can be used as a logical read, or to find specific solutions to particular ills in the records. However, the effect of the techniques is cumulative, and using a variety has a much greater effect than just applying one alone. Record accuracy is of little theoretical interest in inventory management but it is vital if systems are going to work properly, although it may also be useful for anyone studying the tendency of nature to create chaos if left unchecked.

I have worked with my colleague Elaine Duckworth to create a balanced way of enabling people to improve record accuracy, which has resulted in this book.

1

The importance of record accuracy

- Why have accurate records?
- What accuracy do we need?
- Identifying the objectives
- How to measure accuracy
- Accuracy targets
- Record pro formas

Why have accurate records?

The changes to leaner business over the last few years have necessitated major improvements in efficiency, leading to better communication and low inventories with requirement for more timely and more accurate data. Businesses are striving for better quality in all products, and processes and inaccuracies can no longer be hidden by extra stockholding. The data accuracy problem has become a major challenge. This is an area where continuous improvements must be made and standards increased.

Records accuracy is the responsibility of those who control the physical inventory, not only for their own benefit but also for that of the whole organization. Departments far from the source of the records are making decisions assuming that the data on the records is correct – they have to trust the accuracy of those records, since it is highly inefficient (and therefore costly) to have to check each time before acting.

Gradually systems have become more integrated, and the use of any piece of data is now more universal and automatic. Separate records for each inventory area have been melded together, so that in a supply chain there may be a view of many stages of supply. These could be (and often are) different companies at different locations. Each relies on data received from elsewhere to support the next stage in the supply chain. There is little room for incorrect information if demand is to be satisfied effectively.

> *It is not possible to run an effective organization*
> *without accurate records.*

The development of integrated logistic and manufacturing planning systems (including JIT, DRP, ERP, MRP and APS) has to rely on large numbers of records being correct. Without a high level of accuracy the whole planning process could become invalid, and a large amount of extra work ensue in reacting to problems. Improving the accuracy is a normal, continuous process, starting with the 'worst' records and employing a variety of techniques that have been developed by the author to give effective results.

What accuracy do we need?

What is the problem? If the records are inaccurate and it is not causing a problem, then it is not worth improving accuracy until it becomes a significant issue. Normally it is in fact an issue, but people have learned to live with it. Record inaccuracy manifests itself when:

- there is no inventory available to service the customer
- someone lights upon a large quantity of items which no-one knew were there
- there is a stocktake discrepancy which displeases the auditors.

Often the impetus for accuracy improvement results from financial discrepancies at stocktaking, rather than from operational people who are used to living with the situation.

The need for accuracy stems from one of these three causes. Initially the aim is to make the data sufficiently accurate so that they do not hamper the operations of the business. We always aim for perfection, but in the short term we will make do with 'much improved'!

> *Aim for perfection in the long term but set working*
> *targets in the short term.*

A purist will argue that records need to be exact. For many items this is true: if the number of playing cards in a pack is not 52 plus jokers, then for many games the pack is useless. For some items the situation is less than clear. How much sugar do you have in your drink? The answer may well be 'one spoonful'. The response is unlikely to be either 'I need to know the spoon size before I can tell you', or '23 704 grains of 0.15 mm diameter'. The latter answer could be essential for making a product like sandpaper, but in the context of making a beverage we are not that exact. Why? Because it is not necessary. The user has a band of acceptability (tolerance), and as long as the quantity falls within that band, then there is no problem.

The first objective is therefore to ensure that the accuracy of the records meets the current requirements for customer service, financial control of investment, and losses arising when unidentified excess stocks are discovered and written off.

Identifying the objectives

Once it has been agreed that there is a requirement to improve record accuracy, the first step is to establish the objectives of the development. Then we have to quantify how much improvement is needed where, and by when.

If accuracy is measured by value, the result is an averaging of individual discrepancies across all inventory items. This means that there can be major discrepancies on each item, which may balance out. (The accountancy balancing of stock values is discussed in Chapter 8.) The focus for proper accuracy control should therefore be to maintain correct records at item level. In practice, experienced inventory controllers will exert more effort on ensuring the accuracy of high turnover value lines because of the normal inventory policy and the effect on customer service.

In order to determine whether the records are good enough, the first step is to decide what is meant by record accuracy. The practical answer may differ from the theoretical one. It could be:

- the least number of discrepancies
- the least size of discrepancies
- the least value of discrepancies.

In reality the best measure is a combination of all three, which is achieved by classifying items into bands (big, medium and small) or into finer sections.

There is also the question of what is really meant by accurate records. Is it:

1. Having everything exactly the same in the records as in the stores?
2. A general agreement in the value of recorded and physical stocks?
3. Ensuring that major items have record agreement?
4. Allowing a margin of error but not major discrepancies?
5. Having records that enable sufficiently correct data to be used for the business?

6. Avoiding adverse comment by auditors or the need for re-checking?
7. Ensuring that customers are fulfilled on time, or on time in full?
8. Having a working environment where auditing is unnecessary?

> *Measure accuracy to suit the business operations –*
> *not to suit the auditors.*

The basic requirement for record accuracy is to be able to operate the activities of the company with a negligible amount of disruption from inaccurate records. If the system is poor and inventories are high, inaccurate records may be accepted – although, of course, the company may well run out of cash as a result. With better systems, professional recording of inventory is required and accuracy needs to be good for everyone to have confidence in the data. In most businesses there has been increased competitive pressure, leading to a reduction in stock levels and a greater need for accurate records. At the same time, the number of people available for controlling and checking has been reduced.

One of the major causes of panic in inventory management arises when the store is empty but the record says there are still plenty of goods. For the distribution chain, the identification of which goods are available and provided to each customer can be a challenge. For manufacturers, the mis-recording of batch quantities means that they are constantly overriding the plan, so the capacity planning and shop priorities are not defined properly. In the worst cases, the whole system becomes driven by shortage lists – all because the records are not good enough.

Of the options suggested above, the required accuracy option (5) is probably the best. Option (1) is overkill, and option (6) might be good enough for the shareholders, but not good enough to meet the demand for a specific item. Example 1.1 provides an illustration of the suitability of various accuracy options.

Example 1.1

A builder's merchant had a wide variety of stocks to be managed, one of which was sand, which was bought by the lorry load and sold by the bag. Examining the heap was not very helpful in defining the amount in stock, since the weight and shape of the heap depended on whether it had rained recently; the weight delivered varied for the same reason. The process of issuing sand was either to use a spade to fill a bag until it was almost full, or to load a scoopful onto a lorry with a mechanical digger. All these processes were very inexact, and yet there was no problem with stocks of sand.

From a theoretical point of view, it would be good to have 'accurate' records. This could mean:

- *to the nearest sand heap (which is too inexact)*
- *to the nearest digger scoopful (which is a bit of a coarse measure)*
- *to the nearest spadeful (which would be ideal)*
- *to the nearest grain (which would be impractical).*

It would be possible to devise ways to gain tight control over the stock of sand – for example by:

- *controlling the water content of sand purchased*
- *measuring the volumes accurately*
- *storing the sand under cover*
- *using standard bags for issue, not recycled ones*
- *segregating deliveries*
- *storing the sand in hoppers.*

Using these methods successfully would give better control, but would there be a benefit to the business? Here, the benefits would be:

- *a reduction in the total amount of sand stocked*
- *the ability to use recorded stock instead of physical inspection.*

The value of the benefits would clearly be very low in this case, but the cost of improvements would be relatively high in terms of capital cost and operating time for this particular location. The stock control was therefore considered adequate for the application, and no major changes were introduced. However, there were some simple changes made in location, facilities and organization which gave small improvements to the control of stock, and which may gradually improve recording and control.

How to measure accuracy

The principle to adopt is to have records where accuracy is high enough to be very satisfactory for the users, but without wasting resources on minuscule differences. The approach used for the heap of sand in the above example would have been somewhat different if the material in question were gold dust! It is very likely that, having improved the accuracy of records, other aspects of the operations can also be improved. As a result there is a benefit to efficiency, and the onus is again to gain greater accuracy.

> *Maintain a quantitative measure of accuracy.*

It is stated that, for successful operation of the closed-loop systems for supply and control of inventory (including ERP), records have to be 95 per cent accurate. What does this mean, and how should it be measured?

The measurement of record accuracy should be based upon the focus of interest (see (1) to (8) above). The specific measurements can be based on:

- value inaccuracy
- problems arising on issues (e.g. stockouts)
- stock-check discrepancies.

In our measurement of availability for customers (delivery-on-time performance), analysis should identify the proportion of stockouts that are caused by inaccurate records. This is the important measure, since it focuses on the items that are really required by the customers – and thus will have the most detrimental effect on the business.

More commonly, accuracy is measured by discrepancies during stock checking – especially if perpetual inventory checking is being carried out (for a discussion of perpetual inventory checking, see Chapter 9).

The ultimate is to have 100 per cent accuracy during stock checks. What is 100 per cent accuracy? Zero defects. The discussion of the sand heap exemplifies the need for a concept of 'tolerance'. When measuring or manufacturing anything, there is a 'margin of error'. A signpost may say 'Picnic site 100 m'. It could be 1 mm more than that, but there is an accepted tolerance. If a measure is 10 m, there is an inferred tolerance of, say, 1 m. In engineering, the 'tolerances' are agreed or stated explicitly – e.g. '±0.001 mm'.

The same principle can be used in measuring stock quantity. The tolerance allowed for stock can be considered as an absolute quantity (e.g. ±5 units) or as a percentage of the stock quantity (e.g. ±3 per cent). A percentage discrepancy will automatically compensate for the problems with high volumes of products. Taking an example where any stock within 1 per cent is to be considered 'accurate', then:

a stock of 40 items needs to be dead on
a stock of 100 items needs to be within ±1
a stock of 1000 items needs to be within ±10
a stock of 100 000 items needs to be within ±1000.

Which is the best method of allowing tolerance is open to discussion, since it may be better to have records that are more accurate as stock is used up (which the percentage tolerance measurement does do). This reflects our real concern about running out of stock. The smaller the stock, the more accurate the count needs to be in practice. (This technique has less appeal to the accountant, who wants to reflect the total value of stock investment – not the risk of failing to meet demand.)

Consider a sample stock check of 25 items, which gives the results shown in Table 1.1. Which is the worst discrepancy? It depends on whether it is value, customer service, usage rate or some other factor that is most important (e.g. item 19 has a 30-week supply lead time).

Table 1.1 Inventory checking records

Check no.	Part no.	Physical stock	Recorded stock
1	16	819	853
2	34	56	55
3	35	34	34
4	54	4	4
5	56	12	58
6	66	1	−1
7	67	1040	1132
8	67	446	445
9	68	468	468
10	71	774	774
11	89	650	661
12	131	0	0
13	234	342	356
14	245	184	200
15	320	50	54
16	321	124	24
17	388	51	50
18	456	196	210
19	600	520	500
20	676	644	644
21	729	6	7
22	774	1100	1973
23	811	2625	2549
24	872	87	91
25	983	61	66

In practice, there is a standard approach to measuring accuracy once a stock check has been done:

1. The items are classified by their turnover value into three or more classes. This takes into account the cost and usage rates of the items (see next section and Chapter 9)

2. Next, the size of the discrepancy is measured as a percentage of quantity

$$\% \text{ Discrepancy} = \frac{\text{Quantity on record} - \text{Quantity in stock} \times 100}{\text{Quantity on record}}$$

3. To back this up there is a limit on value discrepancy for each line, where:

Value discrepancy = Unit stock value
$\times$ (Quantity on record $-$ Quantity in stock)

If the value discrepancy is greater than a figure agreed by the accountants, then it is treated as a problem.

(As was pointed out previously, some stock will be greater than the record quantity and some lower; as the errors compensate, the financial view of stock accuracy is more positive than the operational view.)

> *Keep a regular sample check for accuracy.*

The process for measuring stock accuracy is therefore to create records of significant discrepancies regularly, using either picking or inventory checking as a basis (or both), and to measure the quantity and size of inaccuracies observed. These should be totalled by category so that an overall figure of accuracy can be measured.

Accuracy targets

Once the objectives for accuracy and methods of measuring have been established, the criteria need to be quantified. An overall measure of the inventory accuracy should be maintained as a management key performance indicator. This in turn should consist of sub-targets for different classes of inventory.

Items are initially classified in terms of turnover value (unit cost multiplied by usage quantity). Normally three classes are identified:

A. A few highest turnover value items – minimal errors allowed
B. Medium turnover value items – small tolerance
C. Low turnover value items (most of the items) – reasonable tolerances allowed (the majority of items will fall into this class).

(The definition of ABC is given in more detail in Chapter 9.)

The rationale behind the tolerances is that, with a limited amount of time available, it is better to concentrate on the valuable items, because these have the greatest effect on stock value and customer service. The purchase of extra C-class stock (such as sand, if it is not used in great volume) reduces the need for very accurate records without significant additional cost. There are two aspects of stock accuracy to consider:

1. How wide are the tolerances?
2. How many records are within the tolerance?

These two 'degrees of freedom' mean that the results could be viewed in many ways. Figure 1.1 illustrates this, using the data from Table 1.1. If the tolerance is set at ±30 per cent, then 21 of the records are within tolerance, and so the records are 84 per cent accurate (see Table 1.2). This is rather a generous tolerance, but if the acceptable range is ±2 per cent, then only 44 per cent of the records are correct.

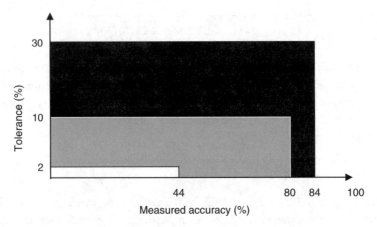

Figure 1.1 Stock accuracy: the 'two degrees of freedom'

Table 1.2   Analysis of sample accuracy

Tolerance (%)	No. of items included	Accuracy (%)
Exact	6	24
±2	11	44
±5	16	64
±10	20	80
±30	21	84
±100	23	92
>100	25	100

This is a situation where continuous improvement is essential. If the tolerances are set too tightly, then so many records are wrong that it is difficult to start correcting them. Thus, initially the tolerances should be set wider so that work can start on the really bad ones and remedial action initiated. Therefore the targets set for accuracy depend upon how accurate the records are at present. The idea is to set targets that can be achieved in the next few months, and then gradually tighten the targets.

> *Set targets which are practical but challenging.*

With the records in Table 1.2, the initial aim could be to get 90 per cent of records within 5 per cent of the stock quantity. As the requirement is dependent on item class, then the targets for stock should be of the form shown in Table 1.3.

Table 1.3   Stock targets

Class	Tolerance (%)	Items within tolerance (%)
A	1	97
B	2	90
C	5	80

The record accuracy assessment is then given by:

$$\% \text{ Record accuracy} = \frac{\text{No. of records within limits} \times 100}{\text{Total no. of records counted}}$$

The assessment can be made on a sample, during a stock check, on the issues, or in any other way. A significant number of different lines should be used in quantifying the accuracy – normally 20 is taken as a minimum, but the more data used, the more accurate the result. It is usual to choose different items to count each time, otherwise there may be a few accurate records and many uncounted and inaccurate ones. It is not necessary to concentrate entirely on the high value stock, since the causes of inaccuracy are probably the same throughout all inventory items and the aim is to detect and eliminate the causes of error.

Measurement needs to be made regularly and analysed each time to give the performance indicator. Then trouble should be taken to find the cause of the errors so that they can be avoided.

Once the accuracy target has been achieved or exceeded for several weeks, it can then be tightened. This should be done either by increasing the number of items required to fulfil the tolerances (e.g. in Table 1.3 increasing the 90 per cent of B-class items within tolerance to 95 per cent) or tightening the tolerances (e.g. in Table 1.3, decreasing the tolerance on A-class items from 1 per cent to 0.5 per cent).

Record pro formas

The process of recording and analysing inventory accuracy should be a formal system. If it works properly and is not over elaborate, then the formal system should be the most efficient way to operate.

The system needs:

1. An inventory checking sheet
2. A programme for planning what items are checked when
3. An analysis of accuracy
4. An action sheet showing progress on improving accuracy
5. A process description of how to carry out the tasks involved and who should do it.

Typical layouts are shown in Tables 1.4 and 1.5, and Figure 1.2.

Table 1.4   Stock check record

Date	Item code	Item description	Location 1		Location 2		Location 3		Total
			Qty	Pack size	Qty	Pack size	Qty	Pack size	

If the system is set up conveniently, then the information of what to count, the item codes, descriptions and locations will be pre-printed on the record (Table 1.4). The checker then has only to fill in the quantity and pack size. It is better if this information is then fed back in the raw state into a computer system, which then calculates the total from this data. It is important that the recorded quantity is not on the checking sheet.

> *It is no use measuring accuracy if you are not going to do anything about it.*

The form shown in Table 1.5 should be used to monitor this process. Obtain and fill in the current data, then set achievable targets that should be monitored and reviewed regularly, and reset (tightened!) at the date indicated.

Table 1.5   What accuracy do you want?

Type of item	Tolerance of accuracy %		Within tolerance %		Date to be achieved by
	Current value	Target value	Current value	Target value	
A *Major turnover value items:* (high value/high volume)					
B *Medium turnover value items:* (high value/low volume) (low value/medium volume)					
C *Low turnover value items:* (low value medium movers) (high value occasional use)					
O *Non-movers:* Obsolete items					

The analysis should then be illustrated on a graph (similar to Figure 1.2) and used as the basis of investigation (see Chapter 11).

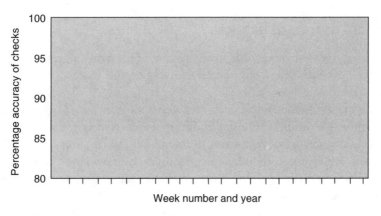

Figure 1.2 Stock analysis graph

Summary

- Decide whether you are sufficiently unhappy with record accuracy to do something about it.
- Work out what you would like to achieve.
- Determine how to measure accuracy.
- Decide what the working tolerances will be.
- Measure accuracy on an ongoing basis.

2

Benefits from accurate records

- How record inaccuracy affects the business
- The financial effect of low and high recorded quantities
- Consequences if inventory exceeds the records
- Reacting when the inventory is lower than the records

Effects of record accuracy

What happens when records are incorrect? Departments throughout the business are affected, from operations to sales and finance, as well as the stock room.

In a fragmented business each area keeps its own records, just as an aid to memory for the individual controlling that area. Accuracy has only become important since the development of integrated information systems. When the data are required by other people, then accuracy is essential. With an integrated system information is used continuously for a wide variety of tasks, and the need for exact data is very great.

Audited accounts require accurate assessment of the value of the company, and this includes the inventory. Accurate inventory valuation is the cause of annual stocktakes, frequent stock checks, and a great deal of effort being put into record accuracy. If the stock value is wrong there are dire consequences, resulting in the effort of having to recount until the records are acceptable. The external audit of stock makes physical stock checking an important and high profile activity; however, the requirements for accurate stock valuation are not as stringent as the operational requirements for stock accuracy. For effective operations, the quantity of each item has to be correct. For financial accuracy, it is only the final value that has to be correct; individual items can be wrong as long as the error is compensated for by an opposing error in another item (see Example 2.1).

Example 2.1

The stock of left-handed widgets was counted as 600 and the stock of right-handed widgets was counted as 200. However, there are really 400 right-handed widgets and 400 left-handed widgets.

As widgets are all valued at £15.00 each, the total stock value was recorded as £12 000. As the actual stock value is indeed £12 000, financially there is no problem.

There is, however, an operational problem. When there is a demand for 300 of each hand to make into sets, the records will identify a shortage and suggest that only 200 can be made. Were the records accurate, the full quantity could be made.

Assessing inventory accuracy by the value discrepancy (stock value to inventory count value) is not a good way of defining the inaccuracy. If, however, the sizes of discrepancies are added (irrespective of whether they are up or down), then this value error becomes an excellent measure. The effect of record inaccuracy in stock systems leads directly to stockouts, and in the longer term this usually leads to general overstocking in an attempt to minimize the risks of the inaccuracy.

> *Inaccuracy costs us all – customers, suppliers and ourselves.*

For manufacturing Material Requirements Planning (MRP) systems the effects of poor records are much more extreme, because the inventory is only sufficient to fulfil immediate demand. A deficiency in quantity causes an immediate shortfall, since MRP makes full use of all the inventory. Difficulties in success with MRP are most often caused through low accuracy of stock records.

In industries where record keeping is inaccurate, demand is often altered at the last minute, and shortages – or indeed excesses – are found, which change the immediate supply priorities. This causes problems for suppliers and ultimately causes them to increase their stock levels and their costs. In some cases this is compounded by the extra work of rescheduling and the costs of extra deliveries.

Counting the cost of inaccuracy

Accuracy affects the ability both to achieve good customer service and to keep costs low. If record accuracy is to be treated seriously then the case has to be made that it has a significant effect on the business – and this is unlikely to be a beneficial effect. This case has to be proven to give priority to work on accuracy. This should not be difficult, because the inaccuracy has a detrimental effect on both customer service and operating costs – and inaccuracy can be a major cost.

Some effects of inaccuracy can be quantified easily (e.g. the extra delivery costs for supplying when a shortage is discovered). Some are much more difficult, but can be guessed at (e.g. the loss of business due to customers losing confidence in stock availability when records are bad).

There are three types of effects arising from stock discrepancies:

1. The results of physical stock being lower than the records
2. The results of physical stock being higher than the records
3. Actions taken as a result of any inaccuracy.

These lead to different sorts of costs.

Physical stock lower than the records

The costs arising from this situation are, of course:

- failure to meet customer demand, leading to loss of profit and 'contribution'
- time taken in dealing with a potentially unhappy customer
- a higher purchase price through focusing on delivery rather than cost
- additional transport costs
- personnel working extra hours (overtime) in dealing with the situation
- contractual costs imposed by customers for late delivery
- damage to reputation and therefore loss of market share.

There are obviously other causes for these situations, so when the real costs are being estimated, only the portion of these costs arising from record inaccuracy should be assessed.

Physical inventory higher than the records

If the actual inventory is greater than the recorded stock, then there is not an immediate problem and inventory availability is fine. The difficulties arise because of cash flow, space and obsolescence. Costs include:

- the original purchase of items that are not available for sale because nobody knows they are there

- inventory holding for unrecorded items (financing and operating costs)
- extra space taken up by unidentified inventory
- disposing of excess or obsolete items.

Again, there are other causes of excess inventory and write-offs, and only that element of cost associated with discovered useless stock should be included in this assessment.

> *Action on improving accuracy will only happen if you can show it is a significant cost to the business.*

Actions taken as a result of any inaccuracy

Whether the records are high or low, there are some basic costs that will occur and should therefore be included in any assessment of the total cost. These can be broadly split into five types of activity:

1. *Reconciliation time.* Where there are inaccurate data, extra time is spent in recounting.
2. *Extra stock checks.* In businesses where data are inaccurate, more frequent stock checking is required.
3. *Avoiding using the data.* There is often an informal system operating where individuals go and check the physical stock because they do not trust the records. This can be an enormous waste of time because so many people are doing it.
4. *Corrective action.* As a result of discrepancies, management time is spent in discussing the situation and taking action as a result. This may be in the form of more frequent checks (which is definitely not the best answer), avoiding the blame, or creating changes that will avoid the problem in future.
5. *Audit.* Where records are poor the external financial auditors will need to examine the inventory value in more detail, and so the cost of annual audits will be greater.

Some of the costs of inaccuracy can be analysed in some detail. Taking the two areas of purchasing and manufacturing as examples, the individual elements of inefficiency can be reviewed (see Example 2.2).

Example 2.2

Purchasing has additional costs through:

- buying on availability, not price
- paying fast delivery premiums or partial deliveries
- purchasing items that are already in stock
- rescheduling as a result of discrepancies
- reacting to panics and disposing of excesses, which are time-consuming activities.

Similarly, *manufacturing* will have additional costs arising from:

- split batches, involving extra set-up costs and complications with paperwork and batch tracking
- rush jobs, involving extra set-up costs and overtime working
- changes in priority, needing progress chasers, extra production control and manual paperwork
- obsolete items that are left because of overproduction
- management involvement (in cost of not managing other topics).

Estimation of the likely costs is important, as this will illustrate that there is a surprising amount of money wasted as a result of inventory inaccuracy. It is then clear that the improvement of accuracy warrants a greater amount of effort.

It is very important to have a quantitative financial analysis of the costs, which will then be used for:

- assessing the viability of devoting money to improvements in accuracy
- identifying where to improve accuracy first
- showing the workforce the penalties of poor reporting
- justifying any capital expenditure on computers, equipment or techniques
- enlisting support for making changes.

The hidden costs of inaccurate records are usually very high, and improvements can be justified that will also provide indirect benefits.

It appears illogical that businesses with the highest stock normally give the worst customer service. This is completely contrary to the assumption that holding a greater stock of each line improves availability. The reason for this apparent dilemma lies in the causes of high and low stock. If records are poor, there may be excess stock of some items and shortages of others. Where records are higher than the physical stock held there will be shortages, and where the records are lower there is an excess of stock. These effects happen simultaneously where record control is poor (see Figure 2.1).

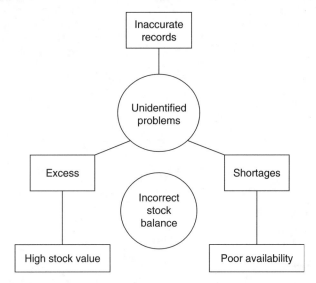

Figure 2.1 Causes and effects of unbalanced stocks

In the final analysis, stock record inaccuracy is a basic cause of excess stocks and shortages (see Table 2.1).

> *How much easier would your life be if you could rely on the stock records?*

Excess inventory

A direct consequence of slack records is excess stock. It can arise from record inaccuracy in two ways:

1. Excess stock results when the records show less inventory than the actual level. If purchases are made when the recorded stock is lower than the actual physical stock, this will result in goods being purchased far too early and stocks being too high.
2. The business has to hold extra stock to compensate for likely stock losses. (However, increasing the stockholding does not usually avert these shortages.)

Table 2.1   Table for the analysis of inaccuracy costs

Effect (Topics)	Size of effect	Frequency per year	Cost of occurrence	Annual cost
Physical stock lower than records: Effects on customers 1 Short-term sales 2 Long-term market				
Panic actions 3 Purchasing 4 Distribution 5 Manufacturing 6 (etc.)				
Physical stock higher than records: 1 Inventory found 2 Disposal cost 3 (etc.)				
Actions resulting from inaccuracy: Management time 1 Discussing the situation 2 Solving the difficulty				
Avoiding the data 3 Physical checking 4 Asking colleagues 5 (etc.)				

In both cases there is an increase in the amount of stock, and some of this will become obsolete because:

- there is now an excessive amount of stock, or
- the demand changes before the item is used up, or
- the stock is not found until the demand has been completely satisfied.

As a result, the business loses money owing to the following two factors:

1. Higher stockholding costs – the cost of holding inventory for one year is calculated as between 18 and 28 per cent of the value of that material
2. Larger inventory write-offs – the amount of excess and obsolete stock written off each year depends on the nature of the business, but often varies between 5 and 15 per cent of the overall inventory value.

Inventory includes all types of items held in a business, within the stores and elsewhere – products, consumables, equipment and spares, administrative requirements, paperwork, materials, and work in progress for manufacturers. The cost of the above two factors is large – sometimes as large as the company profits. The factors can be reduced considerably by accurate records, and even further by using a system that is robust enough to operate even if the records are imperfect.

> *We avoid the effects of inaccuracy by*
> *overstocking.*

Shortages

A stock loss often results in a shortage, which usually entails swift re-planning (and sometimes panic!). When this happens, suppliers or manufacturing are required to provide unplanned items on a short timescale, and normal financial and quality considerations can become secondary to fast delivery.

The effects of shortages are normally more important than the effects of excesses. Shortfalls affect customer service and planning, which in turn affect the collaboration with suppliers and other parts of the company, the whole production planning process and job loading (for logistics and manufacturers), and, ultimately, the credibility of management and the style of the company.

A shortage can be the result of a mislocation, in which case it may be possible to rectify the problem internally through diligent searching of records and stores. If this is not the cause, then external action is needed. Panics come in a variety of types, but the classification is broadly:

- 'Oh dear, we'll have to get some more of those!'
- 'Oh ****, I've got to have some now!!'

(The actual expletive used, and the expression on the person's face, are good indicators for sub-classifying the latter point!.)

In general, stock discrepancies tend to result in physical stock being less than recorded stock, so it is important to have a process in place to deal with shortages quickly and efficiently. This requires authority levels and paperwork (or, better still, IT communication) systems in place to meet such eventualities, and discussion with suppliers regarding the impact of these processes on them. The more often a panic can be treated as a normal 'fast buy or fast supply', the less will be the disruption and cost.

The process for dealing with a stock discrepancy that causes a shortage is typically as follows:

1. Re-check the stock carefully.
2. Find the real date of need (systems often generate required dates which are in advance of the real time the item is needed). Discussion with the customer may establish the true date of need.

3. Identify the 'need' quantity. Often the number demanded is well in excess of the immediate need, and providing existing stock can frequently fulfil the real short-term demand. This gives more time for re-supply.
4. Review the situation to ensure that the shortage is a loss of items rather than a mislocation.
5. Consider the alternatives – e.g. equivalent stock lines and items available at other locations (these could be overstocked!).
6. If the above fail, expedite supply.
7. Ensure that the system is updated to cover any actions (correct stock, purchases and progress actions, customer information etc.).
8. Assess the cause or probable causes of the discrepancy and take corrective action where appropriate.
9. Ensure that the customer is content with the situation.

This procedure will not reduce the number of shortages (unless action is taken on step 8), but it will provide a methodical and less pressurized approach when the situation does occur. Note that 'pressurize supplier' only comes sixth on the list.

> *It is not possible to give good customer service with inaccurate records.*

Summary

- Find the major effects of inaccuracy.
- Value the annual costs to the company.
- Enlist the support of those affected.

3

Causes of inaccurate records

- Continuous maintenance of stock records
- The analysis and correction method
- Detailed causes of inaccuracy
- The role of procedures, training, attitude and control

Observations of inaccuracy

Anyone who works in warehousing or inventory control knows the frustration of incorrect records and the specific circumstances that cause the problem. There is a plethora of causes for inaccuracy. Maintaining inventory is like having a garden – if left untended it becomes overgrown and disorganized; there is too much of one thing whilst other things have vanished (especially if there are birds and rabbits about). Stock needs to be tended, worked on the same way as a garden.

Just like the garden, it is immediately obvious if things are really bad. Simply by walking into the stores you can see this; it is untidy, items are mixed on shelves, packaging is broken, items are left in the aisles, and old boxes and wrappings are strewn about.

When working with the inventory, the results are even more obvious. Discrepancies come to light when:

- an item is not there when it is wanted
- a perpetual inventory check/stock check takes place
- stores personnel highlight the problem
- delivery causes a space problem
- there is a lack or a surplus of fitments, stillages, special transport packaging, etc.

> *Inventory needs continuous maintenance if the records are to be kept accurate.*

The inaccuracies observed reveal the underlying root causes of the problems, and these causes have to be investigated if the situation is going to be improved. It is not sufficient to correct the record without attempting to eliminate underlying causes, otherwise the same type of discrepancy will happen again for a different item at a different time. The process for improving accuracy is the normal approach to scientific or other investigation, namely:

1. Observe the facts – identify the problem, and record when and where it happens
2. Analyse and investigate the facts – look for coincidences, trends and correlations
3. Develop a hypothesis (model) to explain the facts – think of the most likely explanation for the cause of the errors
4. Test the hypothesis – devise an experiment to find out whether this is really the cause
5. Review the test results and modify or scrap the hypothesis if it doesn't fit all the facts – the test will either show the hypothesis was right, or you will need to try something else
6. Implement changes when the final hypothesis is proved correct.

Example 3.1 illustrates this six-step process.

> Treat record inaccuracy as though you were Sherlock Holmes.

Example 3.1

A stock range contains a valuable liquid, which is stored in 500-ml containers and decanted into beakers for use. There is a significant loss in liquid. The results of observation were as follows:

1. Observe	5 per cent loss of liquid
2. Analyse	The same percentage loss happened each week.
3. Hypothesis	Spillage was not a likely cause because the loss was consistent. It was therefore considered that the loss was due to residual liquid left in the containers and in cylinders used for measuring the liquid
4. Test	If the hypothesis is true, the use of larger containers and measuring out several beakers' worth at one time should reduce the error

| 5. Review and modify | The result of these changes was to increase the errors to 6 per cent. The hypothesis was clearly wrong. The action required was therefore to re-analyse the facts (step 2) or even to look for further associated facts (step 1) |

As the process raised new observations (i.e. larger quantities give bigger losses), a new hypothesis was suggested:

3. Hypothesis	The loss is caused by evaporation
4. Test	Evaporation is increased if the liquid is stored for a long time or is kept in an open or partially empty container. The total volume was therefore reconciled on receipt, after storage, upon decanting, and when issued. These measurements were then repeated when the issue process was speeded up and the containers were covered
5. Review and modify	A consistent loss was observed as storage time increased, mainly in open beakers and measuring cylinders. Re-structuring the process (by leaving the liquid in the original containers until immediately before issue) reduced the loss, as did covering the measuring cylinders and beakers. This hypothesis fitted the observed facts
6. Implement change	New procedures were implemented to minimize open storage times, and storage once the initial containers were opened. This reduced the overall loss to 2 per cent

As a result of this approach, the level of discrepancy was reduced significantly. The residual error could well arise from a different cause, so a new investigation procedure is required to reduce the errors further.

> *Discrepancies give the opportunity to find out what the problems are.*

The idea is to use inaccuracies as examples of underlying errors. They should be a trigger for investigating causes. This approach is fundamental to tackling the problem of inaccurate records. Continuous counting and correction is not the answer; less counting and more investigation will identify where changes in procedures will produce improvements. (This approach is also an essential feature of Perpetual Inventory Checking, discussed in Chapter 9.)

Detailed causes of inaccuracy

Murphy's Law (i.e. 'If it can go wrong, it will go wrong'), also known as the Law of Pure Cussedness, applies well to inventory records. There are many ways in which physical stocks contrive to differ from recorded stocks. The typical sources of errors are well known to everyone who has connection with warehousing or stock control. It is useful to draw up a list of all the causes of inaccuracy that could be found in your own company; a brainstorming session is usually the best way to do this. A detailed list of all the potential causes is best, so that the small actions that lead to wrong information can be discovered.

Look at each activity involving inventory movement and recording, and consider the risks at each stage:

- receiving
- issue
- dispatch
- internal movement
- recording
- inventory counting and checking.

The results of this approach can be compared to the list of almost 50 detailed causes shown in Table 3.1. Even with the numerous causes shown, this table is not exhaustive!

Looking at the possible causes simply shows the potential for error. To be useful, some observations are required about the importance of these causes – for example, do they happen often, sometimes, or never? What are the main causes? Fortunately, it is usually found that a few of the observed causes give rise to the bulk of the errors, and this fact enables an inaccuracy investigation to start immediately on those areas that are providing the most trouble, using the process discussed earlier in this chapter. (See also Chapter 10.)

Analysis of underlying reasons for inaccuracy

The many different inaccuracies shown in Table 3.1 can be investigated and tackled individually, or grouped together according to the underlying problems.

The results of a brainstorming session will provide a variety of causes, from the obvious to the ridiculous. A list of these ideas is then drawn up and overlapping causes are eliminated. A quick technique for deciding where to start work on improvement is to give this list to those who have taken part in the brainstorming session. Each person then identifies what he or she thinks

Table 3.1   Causes of inaccuracy

Stock checking	*Quality of stock item*
Wrong count	Replaced not recorded
Wrong identification recorded	Defective item
Missed location during counting	Item past 'use by' date
No location paperwork (item in	Item deteriorated in stock (e.g. rusty)
unidentified overflow location)	
Inaccurate counting equipment	*Reconciliation*
Double count	Paperwork transacted after end of
Item fallen out of location	reconciliation
	Incorrect solution of reconciliation
Identity of stock item	Transaction entered twice
Wrong label (identity)	Transcription error (poor writing/reading)
Wrong number of pack	Correction of records
Identity not specific (mod or option)	• input incorrect number on return of
No identity – serial/batch number	mis-identified items
mismatch	• inaccurate updating from correction
Recording	*WIP in manufacturing*
Wrong entry	Inaccurate counting
• item	Mixing items in container
• quantity	Unrecorded reject/substandard/
• location	reworked items
Missed transaction	Old batches not closed on record system
• paperwork lost	Optimistic counts for bonus purposes
• input error	Job completion recorded but work
• delay in recording	incomplete
	Batch split and part recorded
Unrecorded transaction type	Paperwork lost
Out of hours issue	Job lost
Stolen items	Records of scrap material
Incorrect backflushing	• processed
Type of issue not recorded	• produced
(e.g. warranty)	• specific
Internal stores use	Delay in recording scrap
Scrap/damage	
Returns of wrong item supplied	

are the top three causes, giving three points for the most important cause, two for the next and one for the third. Totalling the points given to each cause should identify what the worst problems are likely to be, and a start can then be made on tackling them.

A more rigorous way of focusing on the major issues uses Pareto analysis or cost–benefit analysis.

Pareto analysis (the basis for ABC analysis) says that 80 per cent of the inaccuracies arise from 20 per cent of the causes (see Chapter 9 for more information). Thus, if there is a list of 20 potential causes, we only have to solve four of them to have a major impact on accuracy.

Cost–benefit analysis is applied in a broad sense here. It is not only the financial investment that is at stake, but largely the effort involved in creating an improvement. The time and expertise required to work on data improvement is normally the critical resource. Some aspects of record inaccuracy are easy to change, others are more difficult (for example, if the problem is the handwriting on the delivery paperwork (Goods Received Note), then it may be easy in one business to change to photocopying the origination document (delivery note) or gaining the information electronically. In other businesses, this may prove very difficult.

An initial assessment of each cause of inaccuracy can therefore include a view as to whether the cause is likely to be:

- soft – i.e. easy to improve
- hard – i.e. difficult to improve.

It is often more effective in use of time to attack several significant 'soft' causes rather than one 'hard' cause. It takes longer to tackle hard causes, and can often involve significant expenditure (e.g. software or physical stores layout changes). These could be reduced by other approaches to the inventory problem (for example, the problem of overflow stock being lost, or uncounted is often resolved by improving the supplier delivery pattern and eliminating the overflow of stock).

> *Identify where to make the maximum impact with the least effort.*

Before simply deciding that 'better discipline' is the soft option and 'system development' is the hard option, it is better to consider the underlying reasons for the difference between the actual inventory and the records. We have tried for the last 200 years to impose better discipline to give perfect records, and if this had been the easy option, then you would not be reading this book and I would have no cause to write it! We have to accept that there are real people acting imperfectly who are operating the inventory system.

So what are the real problems? Typical root causes of errors during recording arise from:

1. Poor design of paperwork and system architecture
2. Untrained personnel
3. Carelessness
4. Poor information control.

Poor design of paperwork and systems architecture

The principle for effective information systems is that the user has the procedure or system available for use and correct all the time. Record maintenance is usually not the prime job of the personnel – they are often in a hurry and will take the easiest option. The process has to be designed for the busy user who sees the process as a necessary evil.

Systems should be reviewed to see where the use of the information gathering process could be made simpler and less liable to result in inaccuracies. Often complex design of procedures and systems leads to a simplified and risk-free operation. There is potential for continuous development of the information process, and this can be initiated by considering the following:

- Is the procedure the simplest way to complete the task? (i.e. is there a short cut?)
- Is operation of the procedure easy to understand?
- Does the operator have extra work if the procedure is not followed?
- Does the person using the procedure benefit from the task?
- Is the reason for and importance of this task obvious to the user?

If the answer to these questions is 'yes', then the procedure is good. If not, either the procedure or the responsibilities need to be changed.

Systems that are set up incorrectly often result in the operator having to wait for them to work. For example, computer users should be able to access their most frequently used screen immediately, and perform routine tasks without changing screens and with a minimum of keystrokes. The system should also lead the user through the logical sequence of operations. Once a computer has been informed of the item code being worked on, it should retain that code and not require its re-entry. Data that are already on file should, of course, be accessed by the system and should not need to be entered again once the initial information has been established (for example, when an item code is entered, then the item's description, classification, cost codes, suppliers and prices should all be available to the user automatically).

> *Are you sure that your procedures are designed for today's business operation?*

Paperwork systems often ask for information that is either unknown to the user or difficult to obtain. Forms should only include essential information, and their design should be fundamentally reviewed periodically to ensure that all the data requested are actually required, or that these are not obtainable elsewhere more simply. As recording is the basis of information, attention is required to make both computer screens and paperwork well controlled, yet fast and easy to use.

The proper authorization of documents is one aspect of paperwork that is frequently abused, particularly in the case of stores issues. The formal system often provides for a selected list of signatories, and, to provide good control, this list should be strictly adhered to, with a procedure and definition for 'exceptional circumstances'. If it is not used, then there is no reason to have the theoretical task.

An abuse of authorization occurs if the signatory signs the paperwork without sufficient consideration. Maybe 90 per cent of routine paperwork is signed while authorizers are doing or thinking about something else – they take the pen, make their mark, and trust the person who filled out the paperwork. This process adds no value to the paperwork, but often involves a great deal of effort in finding a signatory by the person wanting the item. This time wasting could be avoided if just items with high turnover values (A class), or those that are otherwise critical or important, require signatures of supervision or management, and the remaining items are controlled by total spend by each person requiring items. This enables supervisors to sign fewer documents and to give proper attention to those items that affect the business most.

The antedote to Murphy's Law is Failsafing (*Pokeyoka*). Design the system so that it cannot go wrong. This is difficult in practice, but an essential goal if data accuracy is to be improved.

> *People will take the easy option, so make sure that that is the formal system.*

Untrained personnel

Normally, people using a computer system learn the process through formal training or by learning from colleagues. If the processes are simple, training requirements are minimal. However, there should be strict procedures for carrying out all processes, and these are particularly helpful where usage occurs only infrequently, and to ensure error-free processing. Two main aspects of personnel training are:

1. How to use the mechanics of the process (input information etc.)
2. Optimizing the results (understanding what is best practice, and working to achieve it).

The best way of learning both of these is by formal training, consisting of appreciation of what is being done and practice in doing it. Proper training on the mechanisms is common, but training on optimization is rare. The whole question of deciding where to devote most effort, how to perform processes most effectively and how to prioritize is rarely taught; it is often learnt from colleagues empirically. This can result in poor practice permeating through an organization, resulting in time and effort being wasted.

Carelessness

There is a fine difference between genuine error and carelessness. It could be argued that 'if people take enough trouble, they don't make mistakes'. There are other constraints in reality – how difficult is the task? Is the person experienced? What time can be devoted to the matter? In addition to these, there is the key question, does the result matter to the person performing the task? Consider Example 3.2.

Example 3.2

A simple example of this is to consider a stores issue transaction recorded incorrectly. When a discrepancy is discovered, who corrects the error? Is it:

1. *The individual who caused the discrepancy?*
2. *A member of that individual's team?*
3. *Another team, e.g. auditors?*

Often the answer is (3), someone outside the stores team. This causes delays in making the corrections, and stock record accuracy is less than it could be. If (1) is the answer, it is likely that fewer mistakes will be made because the people concerned know they are responsible for making the necessary corrections. If (2) is the answer, a team member may not be too diligent in solving someone else's problems. For individuals to correct their own records, the procedure has to be straightforward and auditable. There must be immediate access to the correction screen (for computer records), personalized transactions, and an audit trail, preferably showing the values altered as well as the quantities. Normally people can be persuaded that when they are solely responsible, their level of accuracy has to be high. The right climate and the right targets can drastically reduce discrepancies.

The solution to carelessness is to engender the right attitude by creating the right environment.

There is also a personal element to accuracy. Different people have different styles. For record accuracy, we would like people who are meticulous in action, accurate, reliable, and always follow the procedures. However, people are not always like that, and we do need people with flair to sort out discrepancies and developing processes; these are unlikely to be the same type of person.

Ideally we would like to have a choice of the range of personal styles in charge of inventory, but usually the existing team is established. There are a number of factors that help people to perform well. The design of the task is therefore the primary concern, and the design of the paperwork and systems should follow on from this.

Recording has traditionally been a job that is not a 'proper' stores job – it has been an odd activity to do when there is nothing better to do, or when it really has to be done because someone is shouting.

> *Jobs need to be interesting, important, challenging and rewarding.*

From a business point of view, keeping the stock records is very important because of the effect on customer service and the credibility of the business. To make the recording task more appealing, it has to be valuable to the person doing the recording job – it has to be rewarding and give that person some benefit. What makes a job appealing includes concepts such as:

- the level of job skills required (not too difficult and not too easy)
- the kudos from and the status of the job
- support given by colleagues
- the worker's own perception of value of the job vs other tasks
- perceived pressure on time
- the nuisance level of the task (extra walking, effort, personnel)
- interaction with others (getting on with co-workers)
- relative financial reward.

Poor information control

Poor control takes the form of lost information, delays, and inconsistent processing. Again, the process of failsafing the procedures has to be the prime aim.

There are many simple ways to improve information control, including the following:

1. The paperwork flow can be simplified
2. Paper transactions can be identified when they are completed (e.g. ticked or initialled)

3. Documents can be serial numbered
4. Records can be put into controlled locations.

However, before refining the paperwork, consider whether the document is essential in the first place. Questions to ask are:

1. Does the product or process change as a result of the information?
2. Could that change be created more simply, or as a result of other information?
3. Is the document necessary, or could the information source be used instead?
4. Can the system be modified to avoid the use of this document?

You have to have creative answers to these questions in order to make successful changes. The paperwork was originated to fulfil a need, sometimes as a reaction to a short-term situation, which may have changed as other procedures and systems have been introduced. There is always potential for improvement.

> *Don't blame the people – it's the system.*

The ideas just discussed for improving accuracy are simple, basic and direct. They are the first obvious steps to take, yet they are the ones where most businesses have room for improvement. By attending to the day-to-day operations, small changes can be made which have a major impact on the overall accuracy. After all, only a very small proportion of inventory activities cause the errors. Therefore, the solving of inaccuracies is going to result from tightening up a situation that is already quite effective.

Summary

- Observe the situations leading to inaccuracy.
- Identify the major potential causes.
- Concentrate on the major causes.
- Think up a process that might cause the problem.
- Devise a test to see if the idea was right.
- Look for the underlying reasons.
- Try basic solutions first, and those that are easy to implement.

4

Structures to avoid inaccuracy

- Avoiding inventory and improving accuracy
- Improving accuracy through simplifying, layout and eliminating errors
- Reducing the stock levels to reduce inaccuracy
- Using others to maintain accurate records

Low inventory levels

If at first you don't succeed – try some thing different! The way to improve the accuracy situation may not be to work on the control of inventory itself; it may be to avoid the problem instead. Is the inventory really necessary to the business? If there is nothing there, then it is easy to count! What opportunities are there to avoid owning inventory in the first place?

> *Checking is easy when there is no inventory!*

For retailers, there has to be a selection on the shelf so that the customers have choice. In many other situations, the inventory can ideally be kept at zero until the item is needed. The easy way to ensure that records are accurate is to have no inventory in stock – it is easy to count and it takes up no space! This is similar to the principle of lean supply, which sets out the ideal situation and then heads towards it by successively eliminating the worst aspects that block improvements.

This may seem a bit theoretical, but there is an important principle here. There are several ways of using the inventory reduction approach, including:

- lean stock levels
- just-in-time (JIT)
- vendor-managed inventory (VMI).

The overall principles for decreasing the problem are well known. The level of inventory can be reduced through more effective control techniques, including:

- communication
- coordination
- forecasting
- inventory management techniques
- supply control.

The proper control of inventory using safety stock theory minimizes the amount of inventory and maximizes the availability to meet demand (see Wild, T. (2002) *Best Practice in Inventory Management*, 2nd edn, Butterworth-Heinemann). Using the proper control techniques reduces the amount of slow-moving inventory, and therefore the amount of counting. If a significant source of error is caused by counting, then minimizing the stock has a worthwhile benefit.

Often time is wasted by having to count excess and obsolete stocks. These are a result of poor forecasting and inventory level control. This can be improved by better supply and inventory management.

The ultimate technique could be JIT – no inventory, no problem, except that there is demand to support at the same time. On the way towards JIT other options can be considered – such as VMI, where the challenge of maintaining accurate records can be transferred to suppliers.

Zero inventory

The concept of a supply chain is to have items flowing from one stage of supply to the next, both within the business and along the supply chain. Any stock in the system is caused by delay between the processes (demand, distribution, transfer, recording and production). The more stock there is in more locations the more difficult it is to count, and therefore one of the techniques that should be considered when reducing inventory is to eliminate stockholding processes. Eliminating stock can be achieved by:

- linking processes
- making the same throughput rate on processes
- locating processes near each other
- coordinating plans.

Conditions for reducing stock

It may not be possible to eliminate stockholding in many cases, but the stock level can be reduced, and with it the amount of time taken in stock counting and the accuracy of the count. Stock reduction will result when the causes of stockholding disappear. The issues to resolve often arise from the unreliability of:

- product quality – rejects
- process capability – breakdown
- supplier delivery – shortages
- consistency of information – reactive operating
- customers changing their demands – poor forecasting
- quality of communication – shortage of information
- the mismatch of supply and demand, caused by batching up and the economics of processes (distribution and conversion).

Changes to the way in which we organize the processes will give significant benefits in accuracy. The way to make improvements is through normal lean supply methods:

- simplification
- failsafing – Pokeyoka
- Kanban – fixed quantity in box (for A class items)
- Cando.

Consider how these can be used for record accuracy. These form a very important basis for the improvement of accuracy, and should be the bedrock of any improvements which are devised.

Simplification

Where the operation is straightforward, there is a much better opportunity to get it right. Simple processes work – complicated procedures are either too difficult to use, or drive people into taking short cuts. It is important to distinguish between routine operation of a procedure (which should be simple) and the overall process control (which is inevitably complex). By designing the whole process as a series of basic procedures, the accuracy can be greatly improved.

> Complexity causes confusion.

There is a general principle here. Make the operation processes as simple as possible. Situations may be very complex – they usually are – but once a process has been set up, the operation of that process has to be simple if it is to work reliably. This applies particularly to operating inventory (see the stock-checking illustration in Example 4.1).

Example 4.1

Items arrive in boxes of 144, and are held together in packaging in 12s. There is a bin in stores to keep them in, so that they can be unwrapped and stored. The stock record needs checking, it shows 339 in stock.

One of the stores personnel has suggested an alternative way of storing them: the boxes of 144 could be kept intact until required, and the packs of 12 could also be left intact until they need to be used. The stock of 339 is then split into 2 boxes of 144, 4 packs of 12 and 3 loose.

Which would be best for the stock checker? Which would result in the more reliable count? Of course, the second will be the easier one to do – especially if the computer will do the multiplication and addition.

As another example, think about your car or computer. There are very few people who understand the detailed operation of the electronics they are using. People accept that it works, and are able to drive and operate the computer without worrying about the technology. It is only when it breaks down that we need experts. If we apply the same principle to inventory management, then we have to ensure that the systems are easy to use. Unfortunately, we rarely have the backing of an inventory record expert to set up the processes in the first place, so the challenge is to set up the operation so that the daily routines are easy.

Failsafing

The idea of failsafing is to create processes which can't go wrong. (It was originally known in Japan as *Pokeyoka*). The aim is to make sure that Murphy's Law (i.e. 'If it can go wrong, it will go wrong') can't operate (he obviously had experience in stores!).

Failsafing has been gradually introduced as a technique for achieving 'right first time'. It can be applied to any operations, whether in administration or elsewhere. The challenge is to design processes so that they simply can't go wrong.

There are stages of process development toward a failsafe operation, for example:

Stage 1	Traditional	An operator in a production line makes an assembly by hand on a bench. The quality is variable, but this is checked later by inspection
Stage 2	Assisted	The operator is given a jig so that he or she can assemble the unit more accurately, thus giving a much lower rate of reject
Stage 3	Self-checking	The operator inserts the item into a tester after assembly, and therefore gets immediate feedback about any defect and can rectify it immediately
Stage 4	Failsafed?	The operator uses an assembly rig where all the items are located and there is no margin for error. The tester is used but doesn't find any defects. The management team is trying to decide whether to stop testing or whether to tighten the tolerances to get a higher quality product

There are some processes that are intrinsically reliable (photocopying, data transmission) and some that are intrinsically risky (writing, remembering, typing). For a system to work accurately, it must include reliable processes. For example, if we are 99 per cent accurate in recording movements through a stores and the average item is moved 10 times (including receiving, transfer and dispatch), then almost one in 20 of the records (9.6 per cent) will be wrong.

The principle applies to the recording processes just as much as to the physical inventory.

> Design the recording process so it is bound
> to be correct.

Pokeyoka is a concept that should be applied throughout the business – e.g. design processes, products and systems so that they can't go wrong. The techniques for *Pokeyoka* are very wide ranging, and include:

- colour coding or definitive badging (making it easy to spot the right item)
- copying not writing
- bar coding
- avoiding movement (thus reducing number of transactions)
- integrating quality checking with the process
- changing responsibilities (authority and care for the items)
- kitting (coordinated recording).

There are many others, to suit the type of quality shortfall.

Failsafing involves a change in technique rather than an evolution of the existing situation (*Kaizen*).

As *Pokeyoka* involves operational changes, the thrust of the developments should be led by the operators. The way to make this type of improvement is not to spend lots of money; rather, it is to organize the record keeping with failsafing in mind.

Kanban

Although lean supply has now been used successfully for several decades, the essential procedures are still not well understood. There is confusion between a conventional two-bin system and Kanban, just because the operation is similar. Unlike a two-bin system, Kanban:

- is applied to A-class goods (especially the regular usage items)
- requires regular top-ups (at least twice per week)
- is triggered by the customer wanting immediate (same day) delivery against an agreed demand level
- delivery is the same day from a local supplier
- delivery quantity is one or a few hours' requirement.

All these features of Kanban lead to very low stocks (less than a day's worth) and therefore accurate records. Furthermore, Kanban usually has a fixed quantity in a box, so the amount in a location is either a boxful or none.

> *If the user takes little and often, there is very little miscount.*

A Kanban system operates by the user requiring a small quantity of a major product, which is provided from a small stock (the stock is typically enough to satisfy a half-day's demand). This usage triggers the request to make some more of the items. The quantity to be made is small (under half-a-day's demand). Making this uses a small batch of components, which then have to be replaced by manufacture. These are produced using a small stock of material from a Kanban square – and so on back through to the supply of materials. Each little stock is held in a clearly marked Kanban square, and of course is a fixed quantity, but is low in inventory value.

Cando

Another Japanese technique that has a big impact on record accuracy is known as Cando. This stands for:

- Clean up
- Arrange

- Neatness
- Discipline
- Ongoing improvement.

Alternatively, this approach is known as the 5S approach in Japan (*Seiri, Seiton, Seiso, Seiketsu, Shitsuke*), the equivalent being *Sort, Simplify, Sweep, Standardize, Self-discipline* in English.

The Cando elements are all applicable to the operating workspace, in any type of inventory environment, but its application in manufacturing has provided the most significant changes. Interpreting the idea of the element gives:

Clean up	Get rid of unnecessary items, including unidentified inventory, excess packaging and any obstructions in the stores aisles
Arrange	Organize the workspace so that items can be found and are organized in a logical manner
Neatness	Ensure that any paperwork is in the right location, information is legible and inventory is laid out and stacked properly
Discipline	Conform to the standard procedures
Ongoing improvement	Look for ways to make the processes more effective and gradually introduce changes

The first steps to improving the accuracy of records are covered by these five concepts. It is difficult to achieve accuracy without the basic housekeeping and control outlines in Cando.

Vendor-managed inventory

Instead of avoiding inventory, it could be transferred to the control of the supplier. This does not make the records more accurate, but passes the problem to the supplier and so gets it out of the way.

Where there is continuous demand for an item, the responsibility for controlling inventory can be transferred to the supplier. The definition of VMI is 'inventory at the customer's premises, but controlled by the supplier'. This does not in itself avoid the counting problem, but if the onus is put on the supplier to maintain an adequate inventory level, the problem for the customer goes away.

In fact, the challenge of counting can be avoided entirely if the items are low value, consistent movers. As long as the supplier comes along regularly and maintains a suitable stock level, there is no need for counting. This approach is suitable where retailers are providing shelf space for their suppliers, and in manufacturing and warehousing for C-class items such as fasteners and packaging items (see ABC analysis, in Chapter 9).

The basis of the approach is to acknowledge that the records have to be sufficiently accurate to ensure supply, low inventory value, and at a minimum of operating costs. For many C-class items the inventory cost is low, but the cost of controlling them could be relatively high unless short cuts are taken. VMI is one potential short cut.

> Get the suppliers to control the quantities.

For a retailer, as well as in warehousing or manufacturing, the supplier can provide items directly to the area where they are to be used, thus eliminating transaction recording except for the actual usage. This approach has saved businesses a major proportion of transaction recording and has not affected the availability of the inventory (in one case, the work reduction was 78 per cent of transaction recording eliminated).

When running VMI, there has to be an element of trust that the supplier will provide the recorded quantity. This should be backed by formal, up-front agreement on how potential conflict situations can be resolved. The approach is as follows:

1. *Agree a contract.* The supplier and the customer decide together on:
   - the inventory level required to maintain supply (this should be modified according to demand levels)
   - the inventory availability level (since the reason for the stockholding in the first place is to provide high availability)
   - invoice and payment terms (because regularity of payment supports the continuing supply).
2. *Share information.* The customer provides information about demand and inventory holding, and the supplier identifies if there are potential shortages.
3. *Monitor the process.* The supplier makes regular, on-site reviews of inventory levels for each VMI item at an agreed frequency.
4. *Replenish inventory.* The supplier restocks inventory to an appropriate level. There is an agreed procedure for removing damaged or outdated inventory, and there is also an agreement on who pays for inventory that goes missing.
5. *Payment.* A process is agreed for recording deliveries (if necessary) and recording usage. There is an agreement for payment terms and dealing with disputes.

VMI can be a simple way to reduce the control workload and therefore enable those responsible for inventory accuracy to concentrate on the higher priority items.

Consignment stocks

Consignment stocks can be defined as 'stocks owned by the supplier, but on the customer's premises and managed by the customer'. There has been a great interest in consignment stock from the viewpoint that it:

- saves the customer the investment in inventory value
- assures the supplier of an almost captive customer
- reassures the customer that the supply is conveniently available.

People forget that consignment stock:

- does nothing to decrease the cost to the supply chain
- takes the pressure off regarding improving the flow of supply
- often leads to slow-moving inventory and extra stock-keeping units (SKUs). An SKU is stock at a stores location, so an item is held at the supplier's and at the customer's stores these are separate SKUs and cause inflated inventory levels.

Consignment stocks do not have an impact on record accuracy, since the same amount of inventory is there. The accuracy depends upon the systems and procedures in place, just like any other element of stock. In fact, the record accuracy could deteriorate because the customer (who controls the stock) doesn't have responsibility for the stock value, and the supplier (whose stock it is) is remote from the problem.

> *Consignment stocks don't really help.*

External storage

One way round the record accuracy problem is to offload it onto a business that is professional in inventory control. For a number of reasons (including flexibility of location, lack of space, strategic inventory etc.) many businesses are holding inventory away from their own locations. One of the consequences of this is that they can use outside agents to control the inventory.

> *Why not leave it to the professionals?*

Since this is a formal arrangement between the storage company and the owner of the inventory, there are proper procedures to be followed. This leads to adherence to the rules – an aura of purchase-type transactions, with the associated checks.

Of course, using external storage may well add cost, so there has to be other justification for doing it – or a dire need to improve record accuracy. This is where our cost–benefit analysis (discussed previously in Chapter 2) proves invaluable.

The choice of partner for storage has to be made carefully. Amongst the companies providing storage and warehouse management are those whose record keeping is no better than the existing situation. A few pertinent questions about accuracy techniques, achievements and penalties can soon show how good they are.

Summary

- Before working on accuracy, see if there are alternative strategies.
- Low stocks are much easier to keep accurate.
- Balance flow in and out of the business.
- Look at just-in-time and lean principles for solutions.
- Suppliers may be willing to do the work for you.
- If all else fails, get in a professional inventory control company.

5

Responsibilities for accuracy

- Top-down management responsibilities
- Improving information quality
- Areas for responsibility
- Making accuracy important
- Identifying the items – better coding
- Checking that items are located correctly

The foundations of accurate records

The style of management of a business often determines whether record accuracy is achievable:

1. Is there some inventory for which it is not clear who is directly responsible?
2. Does the management team think that good response to customer demand means rushing around, bypassing all systems and checks, as soon as there is an urgent demand from the customer?
3. Do senior managers miss out procedures and take actions themselves?
4. Is the stock available to anyone in the business, with nobody in authority?

If so, records are going to remain inaccurate, despite wonderful procedures and systems.

The basis of record accuracy is:

- First, organization (and structure)
- Second, responsibility (and authority)
- Third, operating skills (and motivation)
- Fourth, information systems (and quality processes).

Most of the discussion in the remainder of this book will centre upon the third and fourth aspects – operational tricks and professional skills for those controlling inventory, and best practice and operation of systems to mini-mize errors. This chapter will consider both the organizational environment (which has to be right) and authority (which has to be given to those phys-ically in control of the inventory, if the skills and systems are to be of any use).

The example of management

The message of accurate recording has to emanate from the highest level in the company, and has to be stated clearly, reinforced and, most importantly, acted upon. The senior executives have to obey their own rules if their col-leagues are to work to them as well. This is one activity where leadership by example is very important. The role of top management is to steer the busi-ness to greater success. Over the years there has developed a raft of tech-niques that form 'best practice', and all the time these are being added to and adjusted to suit business needs and the capability of information processes. However, what has emerged is a need for businesses to embrace the fundamental concept of customer satisfaction. To achieve this at a profit requires good planning, and the planning does not work if the information upon which it is based is inaccurate.

> Top management must support the administration
> systems – not bypass them.

Senior managers know that. It would therefore be very unfortunate if managers were to override procedures in order to achieve extra short-term priorities – but this does happen if the administration of the systems is not reactive enough. In some businesses, items will still be ordered in panic, bypassing the proper purchasing system, or items will be removed from the goods receiving area before they are booked in, or items will be removed from stores to fulfil demand without paperwork being completed. Managers should therefore take a hard look at the way they organize. If the system is not capable of doing the job, then they need to get the process changed – that is part of their responsibility. Often there is pressure to fix the symptom (usually non-availability), rather than working on the underlying cause. Consequently, a similar problem occurs again and again.

If the system is essential for finding, booking and recording (e.g. produc-ing the paperwork), then it doesn't get bypassed. If the system just tags along behind the real work, and the operational people rarely use it, then it will often be missed out. It is up to senior managers to organize the opera-tion so that the systems are the easiest way to operate the processes, and not just an additional task to be performed by the stores department for the benefit of others.

However, there are occasions where, strategically, priorities may have to be changed in the short term. If the business is organized properly this will only happen once or twice a year, rather than every week. There should be a standard process for these exceptional situations so that the integrity of the information system can be maintained – albeit after the event.

Information quality

There has gradually been a realization that the quality of service, products, distribution, manufacture and all the physical processes has to be high. Processes have to be right first time and avoid waste in all its forms (materials, effort and time). Lagging a way behind is the understanding by people that high quality in the information processes is equally important. The same quality standards that are applied to handling and efficiency for items in the supply chain should also be applied to the information.

> *Information quality is as important as the quality of the goods.*

The situation reflects the culture in the company, and can be compared to the use of traffic signs around the world. In some countries, everyone respects and obeys all the road regulations – e.g. speed restrictions, stop signs and traffic lights. In other countries, traffic signals are taken as warnings, or simply ignored. On some occasions the president's motorcade takes precedence over all other road users. In many countries, the rules are the same but the interpretation is different: it is not so much about enforcement as about expectation, peer pressure and environment.

Administration and stores have two types of customers:

1. Those who require items (goods, products etc.)
2. Those who require information.

What quality standards are set for information given to 'customers' (e.g. colleagues who want to know the level of inventory for a particular item)? In fact, there is usually no standard set at all. In many companies the recipients of the inventory records are healthily sceptical about their information, and will only request physical checking if it is important that the inventory record quantities are correct.

> *If the quality of the information is poor, reject it and get the originator to put it right.*

If the 'information customers' could be persuaded to require the same standards in information as the physical customers do for inventory, then there would be a significant improvement in accuracy. For information standards to improve, the normal processes of management have to be applied:

- measure – how accurate are the records currently?
- assess – how good do they need to be?
- analyse – what are the likely causes?
- modify – make improvements.

Ownership of stock

This is the first fundamental of record accuracy. The primary question that needs answering is, who owns the stock? Each item in stock should be the responsibility of one identifiable individual at an operational level. This should be maintained throughout the time the item exists in the business.

An easy way to arrange this is to define physical areas in the business – goods receiving, stores areas, display, dispatch, quarantine, packing and, for manufacturers, the various production areas. Each area should be allocated to one named individual who is then completely responsible for the items physically within that area – which could be anything from a complete stores to a single location controlled by an operator or a sales assistant. The complete plan of the company needs to be allocated to individuals area by area (including offices, corridors, car park) to ensure that someone has control. This simple approach can lead to conflicts resulting from situations such as:

- unwanted transfers to people who don't require the items
- enclaves of stock where the area controller has no responsibility.

Unwanted transfers take many forms, including:

- movements into areas which are not ready for them (e.g. delivery of items to goods receiving ahead of the delivery schedule, or, for manufacturers, premature issue of components into production work-in-progress (WIP))

- reject items (awaiting decision on scrap, return or rework)
- picked items awaiting further items before they can be shipped or moved to another process
- customer returns (need checking and assessing).

The business should have designated procedures for these activities, and designated areas in which to carry them out if they are an essential part of the business. What's more, the areas allocated should be large enough, and owned by the individuals who can do something about the consumption of this stock.

Enclaves of stock often result because the management team has not defined ownership of stock by physical location ('if it is in that area, it's yours'). Simplicity is the key, so that responsibility for each item of inventory can easily be seen – whether an individual or a department. Those who are responsible obviously have to have the authority for full control, and the resources available to maintain the records accurately.

A company may also own stock that is not kept within its own premises – e.g. sales samples, trial stocks, consignments and service engineer kits – and these are difficult to control because they are organized by people whose expertise lies in fields other than maintaining accurate records. There is currently a trend towards putting remote stocks in a store, the control of which is outsourced to a professional warehousing company. Major benefits arise where the subcontractor maintains formal issue procedures and accurate stock counts. For the whole of stock control, this systematic approach is valuable.

Whose records are they?

It is only useful to bestow responsibility if the empowered individual can then make improvements. Stock is valuable, not only because of its intrinsic value but also because it meets a business need – customer satisfaction. If the stock were actual piles of cash there would be no problem in persuading colleagues that individuals have to take care of their inventory, and the same should be true of any type of inventory.

However, individual controllers have to have authority – absolute control. It is no use having tight control between 9 am and 5 pm, and then no control for the rest of the 24 hours. The authority means not allowing access to their area if necessary, moving items, organizing, counting and identifying inventory, and, of course, keeping the records accurate. This includes the ability to change incorrect records to agree with physical stock. (The audit implications of this will be discussed later.)

When it comes to recording the data onto the stock system, there are two major alternatives:

1. Professional data entry personnel
2. Inventory control carrying out the recording themselves.

The inputting of data into large systems has traditionally been carried out in bulk by specialist data processors. The advantages of this include:

- professional data entry personnel who have good keying accuracy
- a faster input speed
- the need for only a few terminals
- a system that can be user unfriendly to unauthorized personnel
- a good audit trail in case of system failure.

However, there are overriding disadvantages, including:

- delays that may occur between physical transaction and update of records
- transcription errors caused by creating paperwork and then using that to create the computer records
- data processors who may not recognize mistakes in data (e.g. because they do not have intimate knowledge of the items concerned)
- exceptions and priorities which are difficult to deal with when there is a data transfer before the system is updated (the records are not likely to be updated in real time, and the urgency of some transactions may be lost).

These disadvantages outweigh the advantages, and most companies now allow stores personnel to input data into their own records. The risk of mis-keying can be minimized by the system detecting abnormal or inappropriate entries. This problem is small compared to the advantages in ownership and motivation gained from giving full responsibility to the stores personnel. They have the knowledge, and can spot unusual quantities whilst inputting data to a system.

> *Give inventory control the responsibility and the authority.*

Stores have a particular responsibility for maintaining accurate records. Given a reasonable store environment, the stores supervisor is not only responsible for the effective operation of the stores but is also accountable for the accuracy of stock records for the material in the stores. It is up to this person to ensure that the processes of recording movements are adhered to. The supervisor must provide the correct discipline to maintain a high level of accuracy, and introduce procedures that keep effective control. The stores operatives also have a responsibility to ensure that the transactions they carry out are the same as those required by the system or paperwork, and that:

- the part numbers are correct
- the system shows the latest part number or modification level
- the location is correct
- the amount left corresponds to the actual stock.

If little is expected from the stores personnel, then little initiative will be used. If they are included in the team and given responsibility for the accuracy of stock records, much can be achieved.

Locked stores

To give the stores personnel a chance to perform they need complete control, which means locking the stores. Many alternatives to having a secure stores have been considered, but it is safe to say that a company has either 'enclosed stores or inaccurate records' – not open stores and accurate records.

> *Stores personnel should control all issues and receipts.*

The locking of stores is considered to be difficult by some companies, but it is essential in achieving record accuracy. With a secure boundary it is then possible for all receipts and issues to be carried out by stores personnel. It makes sense from an economic point of view to use the stores personnel for a wider range of activities. In many companies, stores personnel are paid less than managers, technicians, sales people and even some shop-floor workers. It is therefore a cost-saving measure if stores people are the only ones who get items out of the stores. If they deliver the items to the point of use, then this is a further saving. As a first principle, non-stores personnel should not be allowed in stores.

Out-of-hours issues can present a challenge. Is the management team willing to pay for out-of-hours cover, for the sake of record accuracy?

This is a test of resolve. Usually, entrusting keys to night security staff or to supervision still results in under-recording of issues. It requires extra-shift stores cover, or stores people on call, to produce satisfactory results. The number of times there is a requirement for out-of-hours stores issues can be reduced significantly in many situations simply by planning ahead and sticking to the plan.

> *The best way to control inventory is to lock it up.*

The stores is the easiest area in which to make the records accurate, so this is where to start. Ideally, as much of the inventory as is practical should be in the stores. However, this may be difficult – particularly in retail businesses, where the stock has to be on display and the quantity has to be visible to impress the customers.

There are benefits in amalgamating different stores together and not having separate stores for different types of items. Larger, centralized stores have advantages, including the following:

1. More sophisticated stores handling can be afforded
2. Workloads can be balanced across all stores activities
3. As all the stores people work in one stores, there is better cover for holidays and absences
4. Space allocation is more flexible.

The reason that all stores are not centralized, apart from parochial considerations, is either that the stores are located near the point of use to improve efficiency, or because expert knowledge of items is required by stores personnel to compensate for poor systems. The best option is to have centralized stores, and to incorporate the specialist stock operations (including goods receiving and dispatch) within the stores activities. Where stock is outside stores, then control is often more difficult. There is a series of principles for use by people controlling the inventory in their area – they must:

- record accurately the quantity of parts in their areas
- ensure that the physical quantity agrees with the computer records
- move items to stores or other areas as soon as they are completed
- make decisions rapidly on any reject or scrap and get action on these
- maintain a tidy area so that material handling is simple

- avoid splitting batches of work in processes or in transit unless it is essential
- have leading operators in their area to share the responsibility for the points above.

The improvement of record accuracy for items on the move (for example in a factory) is often much more difficult than in the well-controlled and relatively slower moving (from an inventory point of view) environment of stores. Following these basic principles gives the fundamentals, while the addition of policies and systems as described in the following chapters will make success easier.

The people factor

When it comes down to basics, the accuracy of stock records often depends on attitude. The best systems can fail if the people using them are ineffective, while the worst systems can produce good results if the people using them are prepared to work long, hard hours and take care that the business can be run despite the system's shortcomings. It is also easy to see that generally people are contented with the way they work, or at least they are suspicious of change. Experience tells them that change often caused more demands on their time.

Some ground rules in making changes should be kept in mind for accuracy to be improved successfully:

1. Simplification of operating procedures is the key – people don't want more work
2. Complexity can be built into systems and software as long as it does not affect the users
3. Avoid adding tasks and paperwork
4. People respond badly if they are asked to do extra work, especially if it is not considered essential
5. People who carry out tasks should gain some benefit from them – self-interest is an incentive
6. Individuals need to be confident that any change in procedures or systems will work
7. Systems should be generic – avoid special situations, and a properly built general system will cope with these.

> *Make it easier to use the systems than to avoid using them.*

Motivation

Some managers complain that their staff are not motivated. What can be done about apathy? This attitude can result from the relationship between the company, the task and the individual. To check on this, it is necessary to consider the individual's reasons for working – apart from the obvious requirement of money. Time at work fulfils basic social needs. What do the people want out of their work?

- security – a job for life and prospects
- no hassle – a simple mechanical existence with no surprises
- low boredom – a good variety of work
- achievement – setting and exceeding targets
- recognition – acknowledgement by others
- job satisfaction – to reinforce self esteem and enthusiasm
- community – interaction with colleagues.

These personal objectives can, of course, be of benefit or detriment to the business. The improvement in record accuracy will be achieved by directing these needs to coincide with the requirements for correct data. Specifically, people whose main attribute is knowing where everything is, or remembering every part number, need to be developed. These skills, although useful, can block the development of accurate and reliable inventory records. (Memories occasionally give the wrong answer, and are not available at all times for others to use.)

> *Find out what individuals want out of their jobs.*

For example, the achievement of 'no hassle' can sometimes be reached by not bothering to complete the paperwork. This saves a task, and other people rush around to sort out the situation – 'This keeps them off my back. The occasional row is much less hassle than all this stock recording.' The answer is, of course, to make the recording process very simple to do and difficult to avoid, whilst the nuisance value of having to correct it and the bother this causes to the individual should be high.

The recording system

When trying to improve record accuracy, an easy option is always to add more records, procedures, cross checks, controls and paperwork. This process often introduces hurdles, which can lead to a disproportionate amount of administration and little improvement in record accuracy. The procedures may be complex, and resourceful people then bypass the system in order to get their work done quickly. A balance must be maintained between lack of essential information and overkill through excessive information processing.

For example, it is essential that movements in and out of stores are recorded and there are few situations where this can be avoided. In some businesses items are individually serial numbered, even though they are identical, which gives the option of a much higher level of control. It can, however, cause great problems in stores if the correct serial number has to be selected and tracked. Reconciling discrepancies can take much valuable time, and it is therefore important to avoid the routine use of serial numbering in stock control unless it is essential, while maintaining it where it is useful for other activities – such as warranty checks, or identifying fraud.

The stock-recording system can be manual, spreadsheet-based or software system-based. Manual systems are more prone to error, but they have informality, which is sometimes an advantage. There are very few situations where manual systems are to be recommended over a computer solution. Spreadsheets are easy to set up, and the historical records are a spreadsheet type of layout anyway. However, the systems can be somewhat unreliable because the data can be overwritten by accident and historical records thereby corrupted. Therefore, proper inventory management systems are recommended. Efficient computer systems will enable wide use of the data throughout the business, and exception reporting at minimal extra effort. Systems fall into two main categories:

1. Inventory recording, which is basically a historic record of transactions and stock balances (good stock-recording systems will have perpetual inventory-counting modules).
2. Inventory management, which is taking the data from stock recording and using it to optimize the inventory, trigger orders, and manage customer service (for further information, see Wild, T. (2002) *Best Practice in Inventory Management*, 2nd edn, Butterworth-Heinemann). Included in the inventory recording process has to be the procedures, and also checks to match the recorded quantity with the physical quantity. The opportunities afforded by high technology can almost eliminate stock discrepancies.

The system must include a simple record of what is in stock. If the system is linked to a basic financial package where invoices are raised as a result of stock issues, then the transaction has to be carried out at the same time as stock leaves the stores, and not after delivery has been accepted by the customer.

The stock-recording system should also include a good location system so that the items can be found. It is then possible rapidly to reconcile the records with the actual amount of inventory on hand. The basis of a material recording system is to show:

- the exact nature of the item
- the number that exist in the company
- where they are.

The 'exact nature' of the item includes:

- what the item is
- its modification, material, colour, revision level, etc.
- its state of completeness (packaged, labelled, finished)
- the quality of the item (whether good or defective, etc.).

The identity code for the item should identify uniquely that the item fulfils the customer requirement. It should indicate the modification, material and colour of the item. The variations in presentation of the item (packaging etc.) should normally give the item a different part number (as it has different components), while the state of completeness or repair should be recorded as a separate attribute of the item.

The location record should enable an individual to find items without hunting, and a good recording system will identify the quantity of a stock line in each location. When items are received into stores, they should be included in the stock records. However, because they are not yet given a location, the record should identify that they are in the receiving area. Subsequently, when they are put away, the location should be recorded as a separate transaction. If there are significant delays, the physical stock in the location will not agree with the recorded stock and inventory checking will lead to inaccuracies being created.

Item identity

Each item held in stores needs to be easily identifiable by people and computers alike. The name of the item is not usually sufficient, as there may be a variety of types, sizes, purposes etc. that apply equally to one name (e.g. 'wire'). People can describe the same thing in a variety of different ways – a car can be described as an automobile, vehicle, saloon or motor, or by the maker's name – and these descriptions can be interpreted by another person to mean something slightly different, but with item numbers the meaning is definite. An item numbered A123456 has a definite specification – there is no equivocation about it. The colour may be described as turquoise, blue or green, but the item specification can identify the unique standard colour without any confusion. A code is therefore needed that is unique and will not be confused with other similar items in the stores. It is important that the code is used consistently by all departments that order or issue goods from the stores.

> *If the customers consider two items to be the same, then they can have the same code number.*

This simple principle is often difficult to achieve because different departments consider that they have special requirements. Drawings have numbers: should these be the same as the item code? If they do, it is very useful because a revision in the drawing can automatically lead to an updated item number. Stores have, in the past, used code numbers as the stores location numbers instead of separating the concepts of item identity and stores location. Also, the Sales Department may like to use product codes that enhance the product image, rather than those that are used in the rest of the company. This brings out the point that the item coding system should be applied across all the company – to products, components, consumables, spares and all other items. In this way records of each item will be accurate, as each will have its own identity.

Choosing the right type of code is a compromise between the conflicting requirements of being meaningful, able to be written and keyed accurately, and usable throughout the company:

1. *Meaningful numbers* requires coding that can be understood by the users and is specific in describing the item. Systems that do this (for example NATO numbers) tend to be long and complicated, and may be difficult for non-technical staff to interpret. A compromise is to make the number identify the type of item, and then use random, non-meaningful numbers to differentiate between the specific items. It is important that the items are coded by what they are, and not by what they are used on. Failure to recognize this could mean that the same item (spindle, motor, fastener etc.) could exist under two different codes because it is used in two applications.

2. Easy to record numbers are essential for stock accuracy. Short numbers aid accuracy of recording, since there is less to go wrong. In general it is

found that the optimum length of a code is about seven or eight digits, with ten being the maximum. The use of letters in the code is very useful in making the items recognizable and the codes easier to remember, especially when they occur in the middle of the number. It is prudent, however, to omit the letters 'i' and 'o', as these can be confused with numbers.

3. Generally usable numbers unify the company. Drawing numbers can be linked to item codes, and using supplier codes has some advantages – especially where the numbers are industry standards. One of the fundamental principles behind coding systems is that items are physically recognizable by the experienced stores person by their code.

> *Stores personnel should control all issues and receipts. If the item code is logical and short, there is less chance of getting it wrong.*

Check digit systems

One of the ways in which the stores personnel can help themselves to avoid location mistakes is to include a check digit. This is a number or letter at the stores location recorded at the time of putting items away. When the transaction is entered onto the record system, the same check digit should appear for that location. If they are different, then the item is mislocated.

The use of a check digit is a good audit method for finding out when there are mislocation errors. Unfortunately, having identified that there is a problem, there is the laborious task of finding where the items were located in order to transfer them to the right place or to record where they are. A structured check digit system can cut down the searching time considerably by identifying the locations with the particular code for the location where the item was put.

Obviously there are many more locations than single check code letters, although each location is identified originally with a unique location number. Each location is allocated a single check digit code letter. When items are put away in a location, the code letter is recorded on the sheet or entered into a handheld computer. This letter code is identified with a location recorded on the computer.

If the letter recorded corresponds, then the item is located correctly; otherwise, the person has to search for and relocate it correctly (it is often in an adjacent location, as we know). It is important to put these codes in a position on the racking where it is obvious which location the letter identifies.

A coding system for producing check digits has been devised and is illustrated in Table 5.1. This identifies each location by a letter. The formula for generating these codes on spreadsheets is given in Appendix 1.

Table 5.1   Location check digits

Location	Check digit
00a0	a
00b0	k
12a9	j
12b0	k
13a0	a
20a0	a
20a1	b
22b2	m
29a9	j
30a0	a
39a9	j
40a1	b

Summary

- The ethos for accurate records has to be led from the top of the business.
- Executives should be careful not to authorize or support bypassing the system.
- Focus on making information suppliers giving accurate data.
- All areas, or potential areas, of stock should be designated to the control of one operational individual (see also the section on control areas in Chapter 6).
- Use items codes that are easy to understand and easy to write down.
- If there is a possibility of mislocating inventory in the stores, introduce check digits on the location records.

6

The right environment

- Improving the supply chain requires greater accuracy
- Simplification through controlling fixed batch sizes
- Controllers are needed to manage inventory in every part of the business
- Security
- Stores layout
- Real-time procedures

Failsafing (*Pokeyoka*)

If we go back to Murphy's Law ('If something can go wrong, it will go wrong'), then it is obvious that inaccurate records are a natural state of chaos. (Some people also think that Murphy was an optimist!) So if record accuracy is to improve, we have to reduce the opportunity for error – and this is called 'failsafing'.

This entails a re-examination of everything that is done, both physical and administrative. There is a simple logical progression to go through, which could be, for example:

1. How was it possible to lose the item?
2. How did it get lost?
3. What steps can be undertaken to ensure that it doesn't happen again?

Step (3) has nothing to do with discipline; it involves designing the process so that it can't go wrong – eliminating the people factor, since people occasionally get things wrong if there is the opportunity. (For example, instead of jumbling 144 items in a crate, there is pre-formed packaging that takes 12 rows of 12 items. Does this improve the chances that there are 144 in to start with, and of observing that there are none lost when moving them from place to place? It is much better, but there may still be potential for loss, so further risks could be eliminated by having lockable containers or introducing other changes.)

Failsafing (*Pokeyoka*) is a concept that can be applied throughout the business. It is up to the management team to ensure that personnel are not put into a risk situation where they can make mistakes. The failsafing for inventory accuracy has to be applied to both physical inventory and information processes.

It is often easier to work out how to count the items than it is to failsafe the administration. Most information processing is risky – writing, keying in and talking are all liable to mistakes. It is easier to solve the risks from processes that lose paperwork.

The techniques for applying *Pokeyoka* are very wide ranging, and include:

- production jigs
- colour coding
- copying instead of writing
- bar coding
- avoiding movement
- integrating checking with the process
- consistent stacking
- eliminating trans-shipment.

Many other techniques may be chosen, to suit the situation.

There are often some minor changes in procedure that have a significant impact on information accuracy.

Failsafing involves a change in technique rather than an evolution of the existing situation (*Kaizen*). As this involves operational changes, the thrust of the developments should be led by the people who do the jobs.

Question

The paperwork for goods receiving is a nightmare. GRN have to be raised for each delivery and passed to inventory control office. It is a lot of writing to prepare the GRN's (triplicate), and then some of them seem to disappear in the internal mail. Consequently, the computer system is always behind the times and sometimes transactions are missed. Telephoning Goods Inward is the best way to know what has arrived, even though department members are often too busy to find out the detail of what has arrived.

Consider the situation. How would you failsafe this process (given the normal constraints of capital expenditure and costs)?

Flow of material

Accountants think that inventory is a nuisance because it causes poor cash flow and stock. Managers consider it bad because the more there is, the more difficult it is to count and control. On the other hand, operational managers know that inventory holding does cover up a lot of mistakes. If there is plenty in inventory, people feel comfortable – particularly sales people – and therefore this has traditionally been the case in retail and warehousing, where 'you can't sell it if you don't have it!'. Even in manufacturing, people love inventory and work-in-progress (WIP) because it gives them security, flexibility and options without having to plan!

A high inventory level usually goes with inaccurate records. For one thing, it doesn't matter if the records are slightly wrong if there is plenty of inventory to cover it; for another, where there is high inventory there is usually poor control, so data accuracy is very much secondary to getting goods to customers.

> *Persuade everybody that inventory holding is not in their own interest!*

Materials management techniques are all based on the coordination and movement of material along the supply chain and through manufacturing processes, as discussed in Chapter 4. Dependent demand, organized through techniques such as Material Requirements Planning, looks at supply timing and quantities. Throughout the supply chain, just-in-time and lean supply techniques organize the inventory balance to fulfil a controlled level of supply: it is all part of the concept of 'material flow'. To achieve this the concept of 'inventory holding' needs to be replaced by coordinated logistics, and the problems of maintaining inventory records will be swept away at the same time. Inventory level philosophy has to be abolished for the sake of efficiency, except where there are exceptional circumstances.

Coordinated batches

There are benefits in accuracy from having the same batch size for an item throughout the business, as this enables the number of batches to be counted instead of number of items. The trick of keeping the batch together means simplification, convenience and record accuracy. Often the demand is in smaller quantities than the supply (bulk buy and individual issue), and in this case it helps if the business can:

- leave splitting the batch quantity until the last process (dispatch)
- buy the items in the same batch size as is required by the customers.

The move towards either of these options gradually improves accuracy.

As inventory is reduced, the lead time is also reduced (since the queue of work is shorter). This can often be a result of slicker administrative processes and the elimination of some wasted time. Manufacturing has to be decreased to the operation time, and suppliers chosen who can deliver reliably on a short lead time. This means that purchasing is moving toward buying the suppliers' standard products or procuring a regular supply of materially designed items, and manufacturing has to move toward modular products if the customer is still going to have a variety of choice.

> *The lower the inventory, the easier it is to keep accurate records.*

Control areas

Inventory moves along the supply path, and for good control it is best to have accurate records throughout the route. The first step in achieving this is to identify the responsibility for inventory, and then there is no argument as to who owns the information (see Chapter 5). Each area should be allocated to a single individual at operational level; that person should be responsible for inventory in an area, and all areas in the company should be covered so that the inventory in every area is allotted. Decisions have to be made about who owns the inventory in some areas, for example:

- passageways
- items awaiting inspection
- items in reception
- goods receiving
- reject items
- customer returns
- items stored outside.

> *Make someone accountable for every place where there might be inventory.*

The easiest way to identify responsibility is to use a plan of the company site and write on it the boundaries of responsibility together with the names of the controllers. The person given the responsibility must also have two additional attributes – motivation and authority – in order to achieve the right environment.

Motivation is initially achieved through understanding how important record accuracy is in running a successful business, and education on the techniques and potential benefits. It also requires risk. The benefits and problems have to affect area controllers directly, either through extra work, performance monitoring or financial reward. It has to be important to controllers to have accurate records, and in their interest that the records are maintained accurately.

Authority has to rest with the controllers of the areas. It is up to the senior management team to ensure that the controllers have the power to do what is required. They must be able to:

- move items into and out of their area
- maintain their own records accurately (within the overall recording system)
- dispose of unwanted materials from their area
- organize their own physical inventory control.

The company has to support the controllers by giving them performance indicators that induce accuracy improvements in their area.

Security

A business must decide whether security is worthwhile. If the cost of prevention is greater than the cost of the loss, then it is not economical. Therefore we have to establish three values:

1. The value of the actual losses or potential losses
2. The cost of avoiding loss (security and detection equipment etc.)
3. The value of the loss likely to be saved by the method chosen (this includes the cost of the inventory lost and also the cost of more frequent inventory checking, emergency ordering, and the knock-on effects).

It is relatively easy to find the cost of various security systems, but it is awkward to calculate the loss and difficult to estimate how a change will reduce this loss. The first step is to estimate the loss, which can be taken as the value decrease between inventory checks – although this does not include any losses where the records have already been altered to cover the deficit.

One of the key requirements to do this is for the area controllers to have the ability to stop people from other areas taking away inventory without recording it. This raises the important topic of security. The physical inventory can be less than the recorded inventory if items are being stolen. The vast majority of staff are honest, but in occasional circumstances problems may occur. On minor items (e.g. pens, pencils, tools and raw material), employees often consider taking them home to be 'fair game'. The approach to security should be to minimize the opportunity for pilferage, and to detect it when it does happen.

There are basically two types of 'shrinkage' which have to be guarded against:

1. Individuals acquiring small amounts for their own use, which initially involves small quantities and causes discrepancies in the records. The cumulative effect can lead to major losses and discrepancies.
2. A team that is removing and selling products or components. In this case the losses are in larger batch quantities, and the records are often modified to cover this up.

In many companies the losses are not through dishonesty but because employees take items for legitimate purposes but fail to record transactions. The nearer to retail business, the more likely it is that the situation is actual theft.

The ways of avoiding these losses are mainly through identifying responsibility, restricting availability, and good tracking systems.

Obviously, some types of inventory are more liable to be stolen than others. The high-risk items include:

- small consumables (stationery, domestic consumables, small amounts of materials) which the company may not detect or want to bother with
- domestic items (products or consumable stores that are commonly used and easily sold)
- high-value items (especially if their size is small).

The basic requirements for security to avoid pilferage are similar to the normal inventory accuracy requirements, namely:

- enclosed stores (limited access)
- identified responsibility for inventory
- frequent physical inventory checking
- identification of the individual making each transaction
- operations audit of material control
- links to other systems
- goods inward and dispatch control
- company audit balance
- special security areas for high-risk items.

Enclosed stores

There should be no opportunity for personnel from outside the stores to wander in and help themselves to items. This is difficult when there is a trade counter or other retail outlet where goods are on display for promotional purposes. The arrangement of goods within reach of customers is obviously most important, and the ground rules are as follows:

1. Ensure that goods receiving and dispatch activities are in secure areas
2. Avoid putting valuable items where the customers can easily pick them up
3. Have special secure displays or storage areas for high-value items
4. Fix or physically secure items in some way
5. Ensure that delivery batch sizes are too large for manual handling
6. Know what the inventory quantity on display or in other non-stores locations should be
7. Ensure that stores personnel are in attendance while customers are on site
8. Arrange video, alarms or other warning systems for sensitive areas.

Identified responsibility

The inventory belongs to someone, whether it is in stores, in transit or in WIP. Individuals should be designated to own the inventory, and be aware of their responsibilities for ensuring its security. A process of signing for inventory when moving from one area to another is useful if employed properly. Often, requisitioning systems are not operated properly – the signatory either does not sign the requisition, or does not investigate why the item is required. This is a waste of time, and it is better to delegate the responsibility for trivia by allowing more individuals to sign for less important items and give tighter control on the more important goods.

The problem of using computer terminals has not been properly addressed in most companies. The use of personal codes is an advantage, especially if the system locks out after three minutes. However, this is not practical in many cases. Some businesses have workstations that accept a personal identity card (magnetic or optical), as used for access to work areas in many companies. The transactions are identified to the individual whose card is inserted. If the computer automatically changes to the most used screen for that individual as he or she logs in, this system is convenient and practical to use.

Frequent physical inventory checking

Where inventory is known to be at risk, there needs to be more frequent physical inventory checking to determine when any loss has occurred. This will help with detection of the cause. In open store areas (such as the retail trade) it is often impossible to enclose the inventory, and inventory must therefore be checked regularly. Tight security means that less frequent checking is required.

For security purposes, it is advisable that the inventory checkers are different individuals from the stores team.

Identification of the individual making the transaction

The transaction history should be recorded on an audit list which also identifies the individuals making the transactions. This gives the impression that security is tight, but the best it really does is to dissuade the individual from removing an extra item at that time.

Individual serial numbering helps to unravel the problem when things have gone wrong. It is not to be recommended unless essential for the purpose, because it causes a great deal of extra coding and administration.

Operations audit

If all the physical inventory and records are maintained by the same individuals, there is a risk that they could adjust the records to cover any losses. It is therefore desirable to have as many people as possible involved in the inventory control system. This reduces the risk of organized stealing because the number of people involved becomes too large. One obvious activity where a separate team can be used is for cycle counting. This puts an additional task on the cycle counters, since they are required to be aware of any unusual transactions on the history files and any mislocated inventory that could be destined for irregular use.

Links to other systems

The material control system should be integrated into other systems in the operations – for example, accounting, sales and purchasing areas – and there should be cross checks to ensure that all items are recorded somewhere in the system. Any discrepancy between one system module and another can then be investigated.

Goods inward and dispatch control

Goods inward and dispatch departments can be risky areas in a company. In addition to employees, there are delivery drivers, suppliers, customers and often other people (including the general public) visiting the area.

The provision of a security guard is normally warranted for a large company.

By segregating these areas, both physically and on the system, the source of any problems can be identified more easily and people are less inclined to take the risk of being dishonest. A good warehouse should have physically separate goods inward and dispatch departments. Transport personnel should not be allowed into other operating areas, especially where external transport providers are being used.

Company audit balance

A reconciliation should be available for the total amount of material on site. The whole company can be considered to be a stores, and all the stores, operations and states of the products can be considered as alternative inventory locations. If inventory is lost, then it should be accounted for in the dispatch, scrap or other usage. Large discrepancies may be the result of items being stolen from the areas indicated (see Chapter 8).

The important thing here is to find whether items are disappearing, and how it happens.

Special security areas for high-risk items

In many situations there is a special secure area for high-value items, or those that are particularly attractive to pilferage. The design of secure areas should be considered carefully – the use of professional advisors is desirable, and it is always a balance between risk and cost. The fewer the items kept, the lower the risk and the less the space required for storage, so a low inventory policy is advantageous.

Stores layout

Stores operations is the part of an organization that is dedicated to the physical control of inventory. There are individuals employed to look after the items – to move, pick and record. The achievement of record accuracy in stores should be relatively simple, especially as the items tend to be slower moving in the stores than in other parts of the company (e.g. sales vans, distribution, manufacturing WIP etc.). If the stores personnel are to maintain accurate records of the inventory, then they have to have the right conditions, which include:

- a proper stores area
- appropriate stores facilities
- a dedicated stores location
- an enclosed area.

A proper stores area

Items that have been completed, delivered or even rejected need to be put in proper secure store areas. There will be no control if items are left in aisles or in dumps outside, or are put down at random. Inventory should be in stores rather than elsewhere in the company, such as on the shop floor.

Appropriate stores facilities

For control, the stores housekeeping has to be to a high standard. There should be storage of the correct type to accommodate the inventory, and handling equipment in sufficient quantity to ensure that the issuing or receipt process is not hampered. It is useful to do an audit of stores operations, comparing the ideal storage facility for the type of goods with the actual facility being used and then identifying what can be done to improve the situation.

It is generally accepted that the stores will be filled with inventory (an addition to Parkinson's laws should have been 'inventory expands to fill the space available'!). The provision of extra storage space is not usually the solution to overcrowding in stores: better inventory control is.

A dedicated stores location

The stores must be convenient for the customers served and, where possible, for those who supply it. The stores may be considered to be taking up valuable space that is wanted for other support services and the operations (production or distribution), but the space must be devoted to stores or else there will be inventory awaiting transit and individuals who are unable or unwilling to maintain the control and recording systems. If inventory is not held at a convenient place for use, extra, uncontrolled stores will appear. (As already discussed, the way to reduce the stores area is to minimize inventory through better coordination and JIT organization.)

For distributed inventory, small local stores are generally poorly run because it is not the prime responsibility of the individuals to manage the inventory. Where the distributed stores is a little larger and is run by one individual who is a professional stores person, there is normally a facility with very accurate records.

An enclosed area

It is essential that the stores area is enclosed by an impenetrable barrier, and that there are doors which are kept locked at all times. People who are not stores personnel (shop-floor personnel, engineers, designers, salesmen, and other, less desirable, characters) must be kept out. Excuses like 'I don't know the part number but I can recognize it' or 'I know just where it is so don't bother yourself' must not be accepted.

Issues out of hours should be carried out by stores personnel and not designated to supervisors, maintenance fitters, sales people or other individuals.

The accuracy of the inventory records depends on the inventory in store being accurate, and it is essential for this that the stores are locked.

> *Step 1 for any stores is to build a barrier around the inventory.*

The need for real-time recording

Processes can either be operated in batches or in individual transactions. The use of the batch mode goes well with remote clerical systems where a clerk can get on with one type of task and then transfer to another on a daily or weekly basis. Batch working is efficient in time expenditure, especially where there are files or other information to gather together before carrying out the task. Often there are dedicated key operators for high transaction volumes, or a day's work is collected before entering the data onto the computer. This may increase efficiency, but unfortunately it also causes great problems with inventory control. Inventory accuracy needs real-time records.

> *Real-time recording is essential for accurate records.*

What are accurate inventory records?

A definition of accurate records is when 'the amount of inventory in the inventory locations is the same as that shown on the records at all times'. This is a very obvious concept, but one that most businesses fail to achieve. They have other priorities and procedures to operate, and are not focused on keeping records up to the minute. It is very important for records to be updated simultaneously with a movement or other physical transaction.

What are the benefits of real-time stores recording?

Having stated that real-time recording is essential, it would be as well to explain why. The answer, in a single word, is 'credibility'. Delay means extra checking, questions and communication. Real-time recording will:

- enable people to trust the information on the computer system
- let the stores people check the inventory records in the normal course of picking and putting away

- enable inventory checks to be interpreted accurately without complicated paperwork reconciliation
- increase the speed of applying inventory corrections and reduce the work involved
- avoid sales or operations personnel asking for items on the system which have already been removed from stores
- avoid expediting items that are already in stores.

The organization benefits from improved flexibility because individuals do not having to check on the accuracy of data before making decisions.

> *Real-time systems give accurate records.*

How do we achieve real-time operation?

Keeping information up to the minute on the system is usually not a technical problem; a more frequent difficulty is that the inputting procedures are carried out as a batch process some time after the movement of the inventory. The process for maintaining real-time records is as follows:

1. Use the computer system with on-line, real-time facilities for the inventory transactions (since most IT systems are real time, this is only a technical problem with distributed inventories which link up on a poling or batch basis).
2. Site the transaction recording terminal in the stores or at the place where the movement happens (e.g. point of sale stock downdating for retailers).
3. Get the work booked as soon as it is received, moved or picked. Paperwork (where it is needed) must be returned as soon as the picking, moving or putting away is done. Use a system that identifies items as 'being picked' during the time between the issue of the picking document and its return to the system. Ideally, eliminate paperwork altogether.

There are sometimes technical reasons why processes are not real time:

- stores or operating locations are remote from the main activities and it is costly to establish fixed computer links
- systems are not integrated, so information has to be batch transferred between different systems
- the extent of the network or capacity of the system limits the availability of terminals, and some areas will then be required to be put onto separate, often stand-alone, systems. The information from these may

then only read into the main system on a batch basis, and therefore the users of the main system will not be entirely up to date.

If it is seen as important enough, these technical issues can be overcome, sometimes with simple and cheap methods.

Where are real-time systems necessary?

Maybe the question should be 'Why *not* keep records up to date?' The answer could be two-fold – focus and technical. The traditional business approach has been to concentrate on physical processes at the expense of record maintenance. In inventory control, as stated earlier, we have two types of customers, some wanting product and others needing information. Information customers, both internal and external, have been getting a raw deal. They expect old information and they get it, and in the main they accept it. What would be the reaction if TV news or currency information were always hours out of date? People making transactions must now focus on their information customers and believe that real-time recording is important.

One answer to the question 'where do we need real-time systems?' is 'where the efficient operation of the business requires it'.

Consider all the different departments in the company that have an impact on inventory records. For some only real-time records will do, while others can happily use batch data. This will depend upon the business environment (see Example 6.1). The general rules are shown in Table 6.1. The nearer the operating level, the greater the need for real-time systems; also, the more sophisticated the inventory control, the lower the inventory and the greater the need for real-time recording.

Example 6.1

A company carrying out a cycle count could use a batch system for producing a list of items to be counted. All movements for these items would have to be stopped until the count was finished. This approach is used by many companies, with cycle counts being done outside stores operating hours. A counting system in a real-time environment cycle would not require all movements to be stopped; in the worst case it would just mean blocking movement on the item being counted.

Real-time recording is ideal in all activities, but where this is not possible Table 6.1 identifies the most important activities and those where the business can usually get away with processing records in batches.

Table 6.1   Real-time and batch processes

Area	Process requirement	Importance*
Stores		
Goods receiving	Real time	10
Stores	Real time (all transactions)	10
Dispatch	Real time	9
Cycle counting		9
Inventory Control		
Purchasing routine	Batch – complete before use of inventory and purchasing data	0
Emergencies	Real time	9
Inventory control	Complete before use of inventory & purchasing data	7
Expediting	Real time	8
Sales Operations		
Sales planning	Batch	2
Sales order processing	Real time	10
Customer liaison	Real time	9
Management Reporting		
Management	Batch (Daily exception & achievement reporting)	1
Accounts	Batch	0
Production Operations		
Design	Batch	3
Production planning	(Plan well so can update weekly/daily)	6
Shop loading	(Within timeframe where plans don't alter)	8
Monitoring	Real time	10

*Importance is on scale (of 10 down to 0) of need to have real-time systems for this activity.

Summary

- The better the flow of goods, the less inventory and the greater the need for accuracy.
- Arrange control for batch quantities of each item that is used throughout the business.
- Segregate the company into areas, and appoint a controller who is responsible for inventory in each area.
- Assess the security of the inventory to ensure that pilferage does not occur.
- A 'real-time' mentality will reduce the overall workload in the business.
- Real-time recording is essential if all users are going to consider the records as accurate.

7

Batch control

- Advantages of controlling with batches
- Using transfer batches to improve records
- Batch progress recording method
- Advantages and application

Identifying a batch

If simplicity is the key to inventory accuracy, then the counting process has to be considered carefully. It is obvious that counting large numbers of items causes more errors than counting small numbers. If items are arranged in standard quantities (containers) that are then counted, the accuracy will be improved (as long as the container quantity is accurate). In general, therefore, a principle can be established for any inventory including significant quantities of the same items – namely, 'batch up and count batches'. The method for doing this is very simple:

1. Devise an accurate method of arranging items into standard quantities (e.g. a filled container)
2. Count the containers to give a small number for an accurate count.

> Don't ask people to count more than three or they'll get it wrong.

Batch quantities

Good control of batches is the key to simplifying recording, and this leads to accurate records. In warehousing and retail there is often bulk supply, which is then split for sales. It should therefore be possible to keep a box, pallet load or supply batch together until the dispatch process if it is considered important. In a production process, a batch is a unit of manufacture that moves through various stages of production as one item. The size of the 'transfer' batch is determined by the physical constraints of material handling and machine capacity. This process is most effective where there is an established fixed quantity in each container. The same logic can be applied throughout all physical logistic processes. Discipline is essential in only starting one container at a time (this is also the requirement for successful stock rotation), and the container can be identified as the 'batch'. Thus, the following formula can be used:

$$\text{Lorry load} = \text{Number per transfer batch} \times \text{Number of transfer batches}$$

If several containers/pallet loads/boxes are delivered together they form a shipment or load, which can be identified as several 'batches' according to whether they will be used at the same time or not.

The batch is the indivisible unit, the 'atom' of material control, and therefore it should take a large amount of effort to split a batch, just as it does to split the atom. Situations where batches are split are normally a result either of the batches being too large in the beginning, or of bad planning. Wherever possible, batch sizes should match the size ultimately required. Where packing constraints or order quantities don't permit this, it often leads to poor control and inaccurate records. Sometimes the original batch size is not suitable for other processes in the supply chain, and the processes then have to be reconsidered as a whole and not separately (see Example 7.1).

Example 7.1

A company makes toys in batches of 200, but the final process before packing is coating in a plant that holds 100. The coated toys are almost always transferred to the Packing Department when they leave the coating plant, and the job ticket sometimes goes with the first batch, sometimes with the second. When the plant engineer finds a way to rearrange the jigs in the coating plant so that it holds 150 at a time, the operators load one batch and fill empty spaces with part of the next batch. This causes even more confusion as far as the records are concerned. Maybe a batch of 150 throughout is the answer. It may not be optimal for any process, but the compromise provides easy and effective planning, and fast flow of work through the plant – hence giving a real cost saving. (However, conventional accounting may not identify this improvement.)

> *Take the best batch size for the whole of logistics,*
> *not for each process.*

There is often a conflict in manufacturing. Small batches give the opportunity to sequence product rapidly through all the processes, while large batches minimize set-ups and efficiency (at least they do when capacity is a constraint). We can therefore identify two types of 'batches' – the 'batch' (or transfer batch) and 'load' (or process batch) – bearing in mind that a batch is defined as a quantity of the same item in the same stage and in the same location.

The transfer batch is normally the key control. If only half a batch is moved at a time, the paperwork cannot be in two places at once and unidentified parts tend to go astray. The batch size can therefore be defined in terms of the physical quantity – a tray or boxful, a pallet load, or even a lorry load.

Batch sizes for each item must therefore be agreed upon by all departments concerned, and batch quantities maintained accurately at all times. This means the transfer batch should be no smaller than the process batch. For simplicity, the record accuracy logic leads directly to considering a Kanban-type of pull operation.

Batch progress control

The power of using batches for improving record accuracy should not be underestimated. The technique developed by the current author to take advantage of this is 'batch progress control', which is simply a way of keeping separate records for each batch (many companies do this for traceability or quality control anyway). The batch can be considered as a sealed unit with a batch record, in the same way as batch traceability records are used. Let us consider examples of how batch progress control helps in a warehouse (Example 7.2) and in a production environment (Example 7.3).

Example 7.2   The Dawson distribution warehouse

Original situation:
Warehouse stock records have generally not been too good recently. Take a typical example of the scringe unit type 3. There was no stock until the last two batches were delivered. They totalled 2970, which put the stock up nicely. The usage was pretty steady, as can be seen from the usage data (Table 7.1).

Table 7.1   Warehouse stock record – SPU3

Sales order no.	Quantity	Stock balance
Balance carried forward		2970
SCU01	400	2570
SCU02	250	2320
SCU03	300	2020
SCU04	440	1580
SCU05	300	1280
SCU06	150	1130
SCU07	380	750
SCU08	230	520
SCU09	450	70

The trouble started when customer order SCU09 came in. In theory there was enough in stock; in practice we were well short. This situation brings into play the back-up system Purchase Any Number Irrespective of Cost, usually know as panic. As this was happening frequently, the recording system was modified.

Batch control:
To address this, new columns were added to the stock records, one column for each batch. The movements were recorded against each batch, so that the amount in each batch could then be reconciled. The records now looked like Table 7.2.

Table 7.2   Warehouse batch progress record

Sales order no.	Quantity	Stock balance	Batch 1	Batch 2
Balance carried forward		2970	1446	1524
SCU01	400	2570	1046	1524
SCU02	250	2320	796	1524
SCU03	300	2020	496	1524
SCU04	440	1580	56	1524
SCU05	300	1280	0	1224
SCU06	150	1130		1074
SCU07	380	750		694
SCU08	230	520		464
SCU09	450	70		14

The breakthrough was that when the batch was completed, the record showed the batch end quantity, which could be reconciled as items were picked. For example, the order SCU04 for 440 in Table 7.2 requires 56 out of batch 1 and 384 out of batch 2. If the person picking finds there are 56 in batch 1, then this is a confirmation that the record is accurate. If there are only 6, say, left in batch 1, then the record is 50 too high and this will obviously lead to a problem when it comes to dispatching order SCU09. By correcting the records after SCU04, (adjusting inventory down by 50) the problem could be avoided.

> *Batch control provides information with very little extra work.*

The attractive feature of batch progress control is that it does not involve any more work – just checking that the quantity remaining at the end of a batch corresponds to that on the records. (The 'batch balance remaining' can be printed on the picking ticket for convenience, in comparing it with the physical stock.) By using this method it is also convenient for the stores people to judge whether the stock records are about right every time they pick a quantity. This helps them to carry out their responsibility in keeping the records accurate.

The disciplines required during picking are:

- to have separate records for each batch
- always to pick from the open batch or the batch specified (this is easiest if batches are in different locations)
- only to print picking tickets immediately before picking.

Example 7.3   The Dawson production company

Dawson Manufacturing is maintaining production of the scringe pin, but is finding problems with record accuracy on this and other products. Sometimes records show stock available when the stores are empty. At the annual stock take, the records are corrected. They always seem to need an adjustment, but still the quantities do not tally.

As a result of this situation an investigation was mounted into stocks of scringe pins type 7, which are used in scringe units. The analysis is illustrated in Table 7.3, which shows that there were 2760 in stock at the previous stock take last year. Since then there have been five production runs of approximately 10 000 each time, and these have produced 50 310 more pins. The records also show that 48 620 scringe units were assembled using one type-7 pin each. There have also been scrap notes returned from 1220 pins with undersize threads. Records therefore should show a balance of 3230.

Table 7.3   Stock record

Scringe pin – type 7	
Stock at stock take	2 760
Production	50 310
Built into units	48 620
Scrap	1 220
Therefore,	
Current stock	3 230

Although the arithmetic is correct, the stores are empty and personnel are wondering how this could happen again.

The investigation:
A report into the discrepancy recorded the following:

The annual stocktaking is carried out over a weekend by a variety of volunteers. It is carried out primarily for the annual accounts. For valuation purposes it does not matter whether the scringe pins are type 7 or type 3, which have a different thread only noticeable by an engineer. In this rapid stock check it is not certain whether the stock adjustment of 570 was really valid for the type-7 pin.

From an investigation into the manufacturing records it was concluded that:

Investigating production figures for the five batches showed that the quantities were taken from the raw material issues tickets. Production figures were taken from the counter on the machines. There is concern that the figures are overstated because of material lost in setting up each time and in quality samples and in pins scrapped.

The investigation also indicated that the number of scringe unit assemblies produced was probably less than the number of pins used. There was a box of 510 pins that had been under the operator's bench awaiting rectification for some time. The supervisor also intimated that the Sales and Spares Departments are often down for some for 'urgent breakdowns' or samples. They are not meticulous in recording the quantities taken. The usage of pins was therefore considered to be higher than the number recorded.

Further analysis of the scrap system showed that some scrap was not being recorded at all. Not only that, but the scrap notes also took an average of four weeks to get to Material Control, and scrap notes for a further 785 were found in the system.

Reviewing Examples 7.1 and 7.2, the Dawson Company may not be the only one to experience these problems. It is significant that the errors found in each of the quantities in the sum in Table 7.1 all tended to inflate the recorded value of stock. An over-recording of production of pins of only 2 per cent gives a stock discrepancy of 1000. Because the stock quantity is the cumulative difference between two larger quantities (input and output), small errors in these can cause large errors in stock quantities. Scrap is an area of record weakness, and can easily lead to stock discrepancies of the size found generally in the example.

Having found all these sources of errors in the quantity recording system, it was obvious that the technique needed modifying in two major areas:

1. An increase in the accuracy of recording quantities produced and used
2. Avoidance of using scrap records for stock control.

To overcome these two problems, the batch progress record was devised. The batch progress technique keeps the stock and production information for each batch as a separate record. It monitors the batch throughout its existence, and when the batch is finished so is the record. This is the same requirement as for batch traceability, but here we apply it to stock control. The necessary first steps were:

1. To have good batch control, with a number and paperwork for each batch and batches kept together physically through the production process
2. To provide rapid feedback of job completions or of major scrapping (i.e. over one-third of the batch).

For make-to-stock it is better to monitor progress fast rather than take time in counting exact quantities.

In manufacturing, the simplest manual method is to maintain a copy of the route sheet on the production control system. The route sheet refers to a particular batch, and when a process is completed the fact is recorded on this batch progress record. In reality, only a tick is required to identify the processes completed (Table 7.4). This tick shows that the batch is in progress and approximately 10 000 pins are there. Normally, the important questions are:

- Is the item in work?
- Where is it?
- When will it be finished?

Table 7.4   Batch progress record

Batch number: F184.05		
Operation no.	Operation	Done
00	Issue raw material	✓
10	Crop	✓
20	Mill	✓
30	Extrude	
33	Stores receipt	
36	Kit issue	
40	Assemble	
50	Pack	
99	Warehouse receipt	

This simple record answers these questions. For important steps in the production process, the actual quantities can be recorded to show up any major losses.

When the batch completes the final operation or moves into stores, the actual quantity is checked and accepted as the amount available. With the records all on one screen or sheet, any losses between raw material and finished parts can be seen immediately.

In batch progress control, any parts not booked as completed are assumed to be lost as far as useful product is concerned. This is the reality of the situation – if it cannot be found then it is not available for use, and should not be in the inventory record. In this way, batch progress records are more practical than other records.

The batch progress record does not depend in any way on a scrap system. This is another important advantage – it is a result of using the collected records at each stage of manufacture. Should a major portion of the batch be scrapped, then production control is informed by the person rejecting the items and a decision is made on whether to issue a further batch.

Batch progress records can be used in single stores or in a supply chain. However, they are particularly good at cutting through the complexity within a production operation. Another example of this is shown in Table 7.5. In this case, the quantity and date are recorded at each stage of manufacture. The amounts recorded as complete vary from stage to stage of manufacture as a result of the difficulty of counting the items, lack of care and misrecording. This record highlights problem areas, and shows the average amounts being produced. When the total identified as Batch 1 has been received into finished goods stock (estimated as 1446), that batch is then deleted from the active record (although it may now be in a finished goods batch record). Any shortfall is treated as lost. Investigations can be made into these losses when they are significant, but there is no requirement by the system to do this routinely.

Table 7.5   Progress of two batches

Batch progress record Part 123	Batch 1		Batch 2	
	Quantity	Date	Quantity	Date
Purchase order	1500	5/3	1500	12/4
Goods received	1537	7/5	1583	22/5
Production 1st op.	1602	15/5	1637	1/6
2nd op.	1589	18/5	1611	4/6
3rd op.	1613	23/5	1635	10/6
Stores receipt	1473	24/5	1512	12/6
Issue	1450	1/6	1534	15/6
Paint	1400	3/6	1500	16/6
Pack	1498	7/6	1560	20/6
Warehouse input	1446	20/6	1524	28/6

This feature distinguishes batch progress control from normal material records. In batch progress control, missing items are assumed lost; in material records, they are in progress being completed. This means that physical batch control is very important when running systems like MRP.

Where small assemblies are being produced, the control record provides a rapid visual check on the progress of the various components. This enables better delivery estimates to be provided to customers.

Summary

- Avoid counting more than a few items.
- Control batches of items rather than individual items.
- Keep records by numbers of fixed-size transfer batches.
- Maintain the same batch size throughout the business (or until the final dispatch).
- Use the level of a batch to reconcile the inventory records.

8

Controlling stock movement

- Ways of simplifying stock
- Reducing stock recording through the 'kit' concept
- Backflushing technique – avoiding the usual pitfalls
- Segregating inventory areas for control
- Input and output – record balancing
- Investigating material loss

Simplification

As the way to improve record accuracy is to simplify and make the remaining processes error-proof, there is a variety of short cuts that a business can take to aid this process. We have already discussed the basics:

- ensure that the stock lines are clearly identifiable and labelled with their code numbers
- arrange the items in an orderly fashion in stores
- avoid having stock unless it is necessary.

On the basis that these controls are in place, further ways of ensuring effective stock supply can be developed. Four ways of identifying and dealing with errors are discussed in this chapter:

1. Kitting
2. Backflushing
3. Input/output control
4. Company material balance.

Kit marshalling

One way of minimizing the effects of record inaccuracy on the customer or a manufacturing process is to count or pick the items as soon as the requirement is known – ahead of the issue time required. The process of kit marshalling warns where there are inaccuracies, but does not necessarily identify the cause.

If there is an immediate need to improve the availability of items in a situation where there are inaccurate records, then pre-kitting is a short-term answer. This gives supply more time to deal with shortages.

Kitting is appropriate where it is known that a selection of items will be required together in fixed proportions. The normal procedure in stores is to select the items from their locations in advance of using them in assembly or for packing. This ensures that the items are physically there. The timing of the kit-marshalling process is important to avoid extra work. If the stock records are 100 per cent accurate, kitting can be done up to the last minute and the timing depends only on the availability of personnel to carry out the work.

If the stock records are suspect, kitting has to be carried out in advance. The kitting has to be arranged so that there is sufficient time to provision those items that are likely to be short, which may result in kitting several days or weeks in advance. However, the earlier kits are made up, the greater the risk of changes in the demand resulting in the kits having to be modified or returned to their original locations, or of items that have not arrived in stores at the time of kitting having to be added to the kit at a subsequent pick – which is more work.

The normal compromise in many situations is to pick a few days in advance and add any latecomers as they arrive.

The kitting concept can be extended gradually to make control very easy. The ultimate is to get the supplier to provide items already packed up in kit form so that the control problem becomes the management of a few kits, rather than lots of individual items.

With a well-defined demand pattern (such as a Master Production Schedule), the storage of items is simply a convenience. They are batched up to avoid additional set-up or transport costs. In this situation, the future of each item entering the stores has already been determined by the plan (it could be an MRP explosion or other planning process.) This therefore identifies the kitting programme and kit quantities required. In the best case, items can be put straight into the kits on arrival and any shortages can be identified immediately. Of course, this means that many of the stores receipts will be split amongst several kits for different days or weeks of demand. This increases the time it takes to put items away, but reduces the overall amount of work. In companies where forecast planning is good, it is easy to organize kits and lay out stores to take into account the extra space needed for kits and reduced space for individual items. However, there are issues to consider when introducing kitting.

Will this approach require more stores space?

There is only the same amount of stock, so the answer is 'no' if stores are laid out for this purpose. In practice, it depends on the sizes of the assembled kits and the boxes, and the variety of component sizes of existing storage facilities.

How will kitting cope with shortages?

The system will always have kit shortages of the A-class items if it is working properly, since they should be delivered just in time. These should be added to the kit at the last minute or supplied separately to meet demand. B-class items are ideal for this kitting process, since the stores receipts cover a few kits and they can be apportioned readily to each type of kit. For the major C-class items (significant value, low usage), the same logic applies.

For minor C-class items, the quantities supplied are so large that the bulk may exceed the quantity of kits laid out and a bulk store may also be required. Alternatively, these items are free-issued to the workplace.

Each kit should have a kit document identifying the current state of the kit, with the same information available on the computer, to identify the apportioning of the parts as they are received into the stores.

How will stock be checked?

The normal item-by-item stock check is superseded by the kit check for these items allocated to kits. The system can treat kit stock as 'allocated' and any normal bin stock as 'free'. This ensures that the stock record agrees with the bin quantity.

Where is kitting most applicable?

Kitting is most applicable where the demand is known in advance – e.g. the provisioning of regular demand items for a manufacturing assembly line, scheduled customer demand, or provisioning for maintenance or planned equipment overhaul. Other applications include project work where the elements required can all fit into a reasonable size space.

Backflushing

> *Backflushing is an easy way to record kit issue.*

Backflushing is a mixed blessing for stock accuracy. In theory it is very useful, but care has to be taken in employing it otherwise it causes great trouble and stocks can never be reconciled with confidence. First, a definition: instead of recording the issue of each item for an assembly, the assembly is issued as a single item and the bill of materials (kit list) deducts the issue quantities from all the items issued. This is called backflushing (see Example 8.1).

Example 8.1

The packing department has an order for a standard traditional tea set. All the items are in stores as individual items. The picking list for this kit (KS105) is as shown:

KIT KS105

Part no.	Description	Quantity
CC105	Cup	6
CS105	Saucer	6
CP105	Plate	6
PT092	Tray insert	1
PL231	Label	1

When the items are picked, the records need to be updated by reducing the stock balance by these quantities. This can be most easily done by keying in 'KS105 issue quantity 1' and having the system reduce the balance on the individual items.

The assembly could be a customer kit, but more usually backflushing is used for parts issue to an assembly shop. The major advantages of this are that:

- only one record needs to be updated, thus saving much information processing (the computer then calculates the usage of components)
- the bill of materials enables the correct quantities of each item to be downdated without risk of input errors.

Both of these contribute to reducing the likelihood of errors.
    The disadvantages of backflushing are that:

- if the bill of materials is incorrect or out of date, the issues will be incorrect
- any delays in recording the backflush will result in temporarily wrong stock records
- any process scrap is not deducted from stock.

To take the advantages without the disadvantages, the process has to:

- ensure that the bill of materials is correct
- ensure that the backflush is carried out immediately the items leave the stores, and not when they complete subsequent processes (such as assembly in manufacturing).

The accuracy of the bill of materials is obviously important for avoiding shortages and excesses. In backflushing, only the amount on the bill of materials is deducted. The bill has therefore to include an allowance for scrap, set-up and process waste. This can only be estimated at an average rate, and as a consequence there could be a significant difference between the recorded stock and the actual stock at any instant. For free-issue items (where backflushing is really useful), stores control can be minimized if the waste is consistent or insignificant.

> *Backflush immediately on issue from stores.*

The usage of components in uncontrolled locations (for example those accessible to production operators) are recorded via backflushing.

A further pitfall to be avoided in backflushing is the use of alternative components. This has to be eliminated, or a rigorous stores transaction system operated (i.e. backflush-record a return of the original items back into stores and then issue the alternatives to make the record right).

If the backflush is not carried out within minutes of issue from stores, the stores record will be incorrect until the backflush is recorded. This in turn causes high recorded stockouts and complexity for reconciliation. Delay in backflushing is a major source of inaccuracy in companies using this technique.

The backflush can be a full downdate of the stock to an 'allocated' location, which is subsequently issued when the assembly is complete.

Backflushing should be avoided unless the processes for avoiding the disadvantages are in place.

Input/output monitoring

The record system should trace items from entry to the business to dispatch; there should not be separately controlled records for each area. The progress of goods through the company can be considered as a series of separate control boxes that contain a complete management loop, including monitoring and feedback systems. Each item does not move from one record without entering another. These boxes are enclosed in larger boxes, which provide a wider-scale monitor and feedback control. There is then another size of control box, until at the top level, the whole company is one enclosed box – the 'Russian doll' method. Within this largest box is the control of all the material in the company (see Figure 8.1). A business may consist of the logistics areas only, or of a sequence of logistics or production boxes within the largest box. Also note, in Figure 8.1, that financial controls go hand in hand with the item level inventory management.

> *If you get more than you need, inventory increases – so don't do it!*

For input/output control, each little box is an individual control unit and records are kept of inventory for each item, monitoring input and output. These movements are used to recalculate the inventory within the box. The inventory is then checked regularly with the physical stock to ensure that the records are correct. Each box corresponds to the area of responsibility of an individual – which could be an area of stores, a retail department, bin, manufacturing area, building site or any identified location. The process of monitoring and controlling quantities in and out is followed for the larger boxes, until finally a modular structure for the record accuracy of the whole business has been developed.

By good control of the detailed transactions in each area, accurate records can be built up for the large areas of the company. The overall picture can be built up from the bottom. The larger control boxes are composed of the aggregate inventory from the smaller boxes contained inside, plus any areas of transit between. The structure must be such that the larger control boxes contain complete smaller ones – e.g. logistics contains all of inventory management plus other activities in Figure 8.1.

The simple basic logic applied throughout each of the boxes is:

Receipts – Issues = Current stock – Original stock

If this equation does not balance, then there is a discrepancy!

The stock has to be checked physically to ensure that the recorded current stock figure is the same as the actual stock.

The trick in applying input/output monitoring is to match the input with the output. If less is provided, the inventory reduces (avoiding zero if the control is adequate). As this is desirable to ease accuracy (and improve cash flow), it is important operationally to control the input.

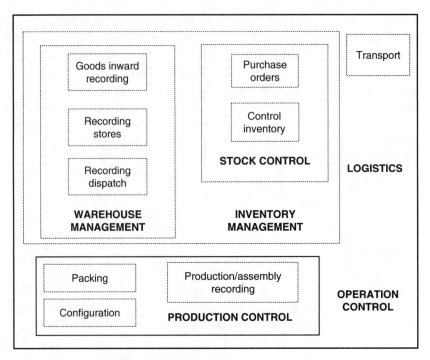

Figure 8.1 Material control boxes

Company material balance

Taking a top-down approach to the input/output control should give a balance for the whole business. We can work out the unaccounted loss from the following equation:

$$\text{Increase in stock} = \text{Purchases} - \text{Sales} - \text{Scrap disposed of} - \text{Unaccounted loss}$$

Considering the balance from a financial point of view, each of these values can be worked out independently from the records (say over a year's time-span) except for the unaccounted loss figure. Of course, sales, purchases, scrap and stock all have to be measured at the same unit costs for the equation to work. Care must therefore be taken that items retain the same values at the start and end of the period chosen, and that inputs and outputs are valued at these values.

> *The inventory accounts balance will show when there is a big problem – usually.*

The unaccounted loss figure can often be worked out in this manner from normal accounts ledgers for each stock area of the company. However, in the ledgers, value is often written off during the year as a result of stock disposal (at minimal value) or stock adjustments (quantities or values). This adds complications, and it is often better to start from scratch and take the total quantity of all purchases, stock and sales at cost or material value than at a standard cost.

The balance is easy to work out for a warehouse where the values remain consistent. Where the stores area is uncontrolled (retail or unenclosed stores), the reconciliation is essential on a weekly or monthly basis – depending on how often the stock is counted. (The counting frequency will depend on how bad the discrepancies are – greater inaccuracy requires more frequent counts.)

For manufacturing, an overall reconciliation is more complex. The basis of calculations is normally material cost (as bought). Scrap and sales have to be valued at this unit cost. Where the process includes the transformation of material by area or volume, there are other factors that may come into play (see Example 8.2).

Example 8.2

It was decided to carry out a reconciliation of the material in a car battery manufacturer, specifically on the amount of lead within the company. The stock of lead material, WIP and finished product was assessed at the start and end of the year. The purchase weight was known, and the quantity and size of the batteries dispatched was known. What is more, there were reasonable records of the scrap recorded at each process. The figure for unrecorded loss was calculated as 10 per cent – rather higher than considered possible. After further detailed investigations, the discrepancy was narrowed down to two main causes:

1. *Loss of items in-between processes where nobody had full responsibility, yet individuals were rejecting items and not recording them (no surprise there!).*
2. *Inclusion of extra material in the products, so that the average weight of material in the products was about 6 per cent higher than the standard. This was within tolerance for the processes, and ensured that the product met the design criteria. However, it meant that the material balance was wrong and the product cost was increased.*

Obviously, in Example 8.2 it would have been better to check all the products out of the door and make estimates of the actual weights. The extra factor in this case (product tolerance) made the reconciliation of the overall balance difficult.

> *Material reconciliation for the whole company can give surprising results.*

Example 8.2 suggests that company-wide reconciliation is desirable. It shows that a project to identify the material balance is very worthwhile, and that the interpretation of results must be carried out with care and understanding of the operations involved. The measurement of company material balance in the example showed that a significant value of material was unaccounted for, and this was having an impact on profits. It also illustrates the potential financial benefits of linking the records together and improving accuracy.

Financial control of stock value

If this formula is used for the valuation of stock over a full accounting year, it then becomes:

$$\text{Value of purchases} - \text{Value of sales} = \text{Closing stock balance} - \text{Opening stock balance}$$

Again, care should be taken here to ensure that the valuations of the purchases and sales are taken on the same basis. For example, the value of labour and overheads may be included as an addition to the conventional value of purchases. The value of sales should also include other outputs, such as transfers, replacements and any disposal value recorded on the stock system. The actual value of the stock balance will contain a stock provision or depreciation allowance, which has to be dealt with consistently in the equation. In fact, the provisions can be worked out in isolation using an identical formula.

Summary

- Orderly arrangement leads to accurate inventory.
- Create standard issue kits where possible.
- Backflushing using a component list improves accuracy.
- Backflushing must be done at the time of issue, not afterwards.
- Segregate inventory areas so that input and output can be monitored.
- Check inventory record balance as often as required – not just annually.

9

Inventory checking

- Simple ways to gain accuracy
- Stock counting
- Arranging a batch
- Stocktaking
- Focusing the task using ABC analysis
- Perpetual inventory control techniques

Inventory counting

Inventory checking is not the way to improve accuracy; only by analysing the causes behind inaccuracy can errors be reduced. However, inventory counting is the essential first step, and a properly organized count is required. This can be performed either as an annual 'wall-to-wall' stocktake (or more often if control is poor), or as a gradual cycle count spread over a year.

Counting methods

Quality processes require counting equipment to be standardized regularly, whether counting is by weight, size, quantity or other attribute, and the accuracy of counting is then governed by the intrinsic accuracy of the equipment and its state of adjustment. However, let us not approach the issue technically before it has been considered organizationally. The way to count accurately is to make it so simple that it can't fail. Counting, especially of large quantities, should be avoided, as it will just cause inaccuracy. Other methods should be devised, and this is not difficult. For example, a stock record of small components shows a quantity of 1024. Consider the ways of counting it and the accuracy expected. The options for these items can be applied to any item of stock of any sort. The methods you might expect to use are:

1. *A straight count of all the items*, although this is time consuming and the result is likely to be one or two items out, even if the count is repeated several times

2. *Weigh counting,* which gives an accurate record as long as the scales are calibrated correctly (allow for container weight, and scale count from a large enough counter)
3. *A quantity count using a counting device* (such as a photocell counter fed from a hopper or other component-moving device)
4. *Batching in standard quantities,* which allows the number of batches to be counted, not the number of items
5. *Arrays,* where all items are laid out in a pattern, usually all in the same orientation
6. *Consistent stacking,* so that there are the same number of boxes or items showing and the same number in each pile.

> As a principle, organize the stock so that people don't have to count more than three — or they will get it wrong sometimes.

Let us examine these in more detail:

Direct counting

Direct counting of quantities greater than 12 should be avoided and other methods for assessing quantities considered. If counts have to be done, counting during transfer between two containers or piles often gives the best result. Recording the quantity after every 50 or 100 can also ensure that the results are more reliable.

Weigh counting

This is often the favoured method, but is not the most effective. It usually requires transferring items to the recording device or changing containers. For good results, the counting process has to be organized properly:

- identify what accuracy is required (per cent or weight differential)
- ensure that the equipment is capable of the accuracy required
- ensure that the scales are within calibration tolerances
- if the items are in a container, measure the weight of that individual container
- ensure that there is no additional weight on the scales (defective items, materials, etc.)

- check the result of the count to ensure that the unit weights and total quantity for the volume are approximately correct.

Quantity counters

Quantity counters should be very accurate, but require setting up and have to be maintained so that they count all the items in whatever orientation they are presented to the sensor. Ensure that the quantity counter counts the number of objects rather than the number of movements, as some operations might not contain an item.

Batching

Fixed batch sizes are good for accuracy because the counting is very simple (count the containers, not the items). The prime need is for a fixed quantity per container. If the batch then consists of a variable (small) number of these containers, the counting is still simple (see Chapter 7).

The equivalent to batching for fluids is to have a consistent container size so that the same volume is present for each container.

> *Organizing the layout of items enables inventory to be counted instantaneously.*

Arrays

The use of arrays is the most simple, effective and accurate way of counting, and should be used wherever possible. The 1024 items in the above example could be laid out in a 32 by 32 array, sticking out of a pre-formed tray. It would then be very easy to see whether there was an item missing, and, of course, only 1024 would sit in the tray. The use of arrays gives the opportunity for very accurate quantity control by simple visual inspection. This is a good example of how failsafing can be applied in record accuracy. Arrays enable a large quantity to be assessed very accurately without effort, because it is simple to see whether the right number is there.

The use of arrays rather than random box loads is the first step in tightening up process control. A major improvement in accuracy can be achieved immediately by putting items on a pre-formed tray. The advantages of this are useful both to stores and in manufacturing businesses.

Maintaining orientation of goods also helps in material handling and in counting of part-batch quantities for dispatch.

Consistent stacking

The management of stacking is another powerful, cheap and effective accuracy technique. If one stack is counted carefully to a certain height (one item wide and one item deep), the remaining items can be stacked to the same height and the stacks will contain the same quantity (assuming that the items or boxes of items are all the same dimensions). Obvious! Yes, and useful. Ensure that the racking is organized so that this is possible and that items are supplied in the correct-shaped packing.

These techniques are very basic, but are not employed nearly often enough in practice. As a consequence, stocks are not so easy to check and miscounting results.

Inventory checking (stocktaking)

It is said that the reason for an annual stocktake is primarily to provide accountants with a stock valuation. Some managers are under the impression that it is a legal requirement to carry out a stocktake, whereas the actual legal requirement is to have an accurate valuation of stock – thus where a company has perfect records (demonstrated by audit sampling) there is no need to check the inventory accuracy quantity.

Instead of putting the inventory right fleetingly through a complete stocktake, a preferable method would be to maintain accurate stock records all the time, and simply value them when the auditors require (which is probably only a matter of running a computer printout). Spreading the inventory count is the basis of cycle counting (alternatively known as perpetual inventory checking). This technique gives us the option to concentrate on eliminating causes of error and on those items that provide the most risk.

Organization of annual stocktaking (inventory counting)

Stocktaking should be organized carefully if it is to be successful, and several weeks of preparation are needed. Before the stocktaking, the resources have to be arranged, including:

- paperwork
- counting methods
- manpower

- systems
- procedures.

Paperwork

The function of the paperwork used directly in the counting process is to:

- identify what has been checked and what has not
- provide feedback to the stock records and financial systems
- create audit information should it be necessary.

This can be organized in many different ways, including:

- putting cards into locations before the count, filling them in during the count, and collecting them afterwards
- using two-part cards which adhere to the stock, one part for feedback and one part to remain on the stock
- using a tally sheet to record stock with a marker (for instance a coloured sticky label) to identify what has been checked.

The paperwork has to be organized with a view to minimizing recording errors. There are several standard methods that are commonly used. First, the tickets have to be accountable, so they need to be numerically sequenced. Often tickets are pre-numbered. The unused and spoiled tickets have to be accounted for at the end, as well as those with recorded quantities. It is also an advantage to print the item codes and descriptions on the tickets in advance in situations where the tickets can be printed in bin-location sequence. This enables the issue of tickets to be fast, and the item codes to be readable. (If they cannot be printed in bin sequence then the time taken to find the cards corresponding to the items often makes this pre-coding inefficient.)

The use of bar codes for stock checking (see Chapter 10) can make it much faster to do the counting and collate the results. In this case it may not be essential to have paper records at all, but the process has to be worked out carefully to ensure that everything is counted, and counted only once.

The techniques for ensuring that the recording at stocktaking is carried out accurately are the same as those used in ensuring record accuracy in general.

Counting

Counting has to be carried out over a short period of time. This requires the use of non-specialist staff, or long hours for those who work in the stores. Either way, there is a risk of inaccuracy. The techniques for accurate counting are discussed at the beginning of this chapter, and these are equally applicable to the counting during a stocktake. It may be possible to hire specialist equipment for the stocktake in order to provide a faster or more accurate count.

> *Less writing and more pre-printing improves stocktake accuracy – but quantities should not be pre-printed.*

The counting process should be made as simple as possible. Where there are standard pack quantities, then the person counting should be able to record the number of packs and the number of loose items in separate columns. The actual number of items should then be calculated by the system as the data are input.

Manpower

The size of the counting task can be estimated from the time taken for smaller checks or previous counts. The counting will be much faster if the stock is well ordered, stacked, or sealed in reliably labelled boxes. Preliminary work, if necessary, should include:

- putting away all stock
- ensuring that the stock is tidy
- bringing all paperwork up to date
- identifying all goods and locations clearly
- batching up items into standard quantities
- laying out any paperwork that can be done beforehand.

The more the workload can be spread, the better the results.

There must be enough people available to count the items in sufficient detail, record the results and check any discrepancies.

Systems

As most stock is recorded on a computer system, the major information task is getting the item identities and locations out of the system and the quantitative information back in. Obviously, bar coding is the answer. If the stores items or locations are bar coded, then the task of checking the inventory is very fast and accurate. Bar coding can also be used purely for the stocktake information as a means of either accessing or reading the data pre-printed on the stock cards or sheets. For other information the data has to be input by hand – giving room for error.

The layout of the input document and the computer input should be the same, to increase speed and accuracy of transcription. Careful design of the process will save a large amount of time during the data entry process.

The system should, of course, highlight discrepancies. If the error is big, then a recheck will be necessary. Criteria should be set into the system to identify that a repeat count is required.

Procedures

For an effective stocktake, the procedures should be written down in advance. Each member of the stock-counting team should be trained in how to carry out the procedures, including physical examples of how to carry out the tasks. The count quality criteria should also be discussed, so that all the individuals have the same basic accuracy targets.

> *Minimize the amount of work required at the time of inventory counting.*

All the paperwork used in the stocktake has to be returned so that it can be accounted for. We have to accept that some paperwork is going to be spoilt, and therefore there must be a procedure for dealing with this when it happens. Numerically sequenced dockets have to be counted to ensure that none are missing – an easy thing to overlook in the rush to get the records completed.

It is important that all stock is counted. We have to ensure that all areas containing stock have paperwork for counting and are counted, and that the paperwork is collected and is input into the system. The responsibilities for each stage in every area should be identified clearly, and a simple tally sheet used to ensure that it works effectively.

As the stock check is likely to find discrepancies, some re-checking will be necessary. It is therefore important to carry out all procedures within a short time span. If the check drags on, the chance of re-examining a discrepancy is lost and there is disruption to the normal operation of the business. The inputting process during the stocktake will have to be carried out soon enough to enable the re-checking to happen before further receipts and issues have occurred.

> *Get the discrepancies sorted out immediately.*

Of course, it is necessary to decide the rules to apply regarding when it is worth investigating a counting discrepancy. The general principle should be 'investigate when it may harm the business'. If the error will affect customer service or the effectiveness of the operation, or significantly alter the value of the inventory, then it needs to be re-checked. If this is not the case then, in a full inventory check, it is not worthwhile following it up.

Principles of cycle counting

The annual stocktake has a number of disadvantages. For instance, it:

- is not very effective at correcting the detailed stock discrepancies
- disrupts the issue of items and can affect customer service
- puts the counters under a time pressure to get the job completed
- causes a large amount of extra work over a period of two to three weeks
- involves significant cost to the business.

The inventory records can be made more accurate by counting items gradually throughout the year. A formal system for counting, usually called perpetual inventory checking, or cycle counting, formalizes this procedure.

Some companies carry out stock checking every year, and cycle counting for internal stock control purposes. Carrying out both types of checking is a duplication of effort. Improvements in record accuracy could be made, through less counting, by organizing a cycle counting process that is acceptable to the company auditors.

The options available for ways of counting the stock are numerous. They can be based on:

- aisle to aisle counting – this is simple to organize, as counters start at one end of the stores and gradually work along to the other
- the number of movements – but faster moving items with more transactions may have more errors
- the importance of an item – critical items for use or for specific customers may need more attention
- the value of an item – high-value items are sometimes thought to need more checks (but total stock value is actually more important)

- the item's attractiveness (i.e. likelihood of pilferage) – some usable items may need special security and careful control
- the item's turnover value – high stock value items need more control because of customer requirement or financial investment.

Aisle counting is convenient to carry out, but the best method in most circumstances is turnover value.

> *Make it as simple as ABC – and reduce the workload.*

ABC analysis

The basis of cycle counting by turnover value is ABC analysis, which is one of the key methods on which material management and many other forms of management are based. It is a specific application of Pareto analysis, which is named after one of the original workers in the field, who found that the majority of the wealth of Italians was concentrated in a small number of families.

To create an ABC analysis, the steps are as follows:

1. List all the stock items, their unit cost and their usage rate per year (or average expected usage rate for new items). (If the information is not perfect it does not matter too much.)
2. Multiply unit cost by usage for each item to give the issue value.
3. List items in descending order of issue value (note that some items at the start of the list have low value but high movement).
4. Add down the column cumulatively (the last figure should be the total issue value).
5. There are some items in stock for which there have been no issues and therefore the multiplication gives zero; these are at the bottom of the list, and should be categorized as class-D items.

If the values of the stocks are added successfully, then the shape of this curve is the ABC or Pareto curve (see Figure 9.1). The total issue value comes from 100 per cent of the items, and we find that in general 80 per cent of the stock value comes from 20 per cent of the items – this is sometimes called the 80 : 20 rule. The curve can be applied to many aspects of material control; it is used for reducing stock value, rationalizing part number, product profitability, assessment of wastage, and utilization of management time (see Wild, T. (2002) *Best Practice in Inventory Management*, 2nd edn, Chapter 3, Butterworth-Heinemann).

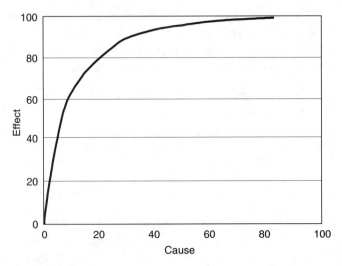

Figure 9.1 Pareto curve

The remainder of the curve is divided into A, B and C classes: A class is normally the first 10 per cent of part moving numbers, B class is the next 20 per cent, and C class is the remaining 70 per cent. The control required for A-class items must ensure that service remains high while maintaining a low quantity of stock, so the records have to be accurate. In contrast, for C-class items it is important to organize correct provisioning and the manipulation of a large amount of data (70 per cent of active item codes). It is not so important to maintain the exact level of stock for C-class items, as it is relatively cheap to hold a bit extra in case of discrepancy.

Demonstration of classification by ABC analysis

A demonstration of ABC analysis using a very few item codes is shown in the following tables.

Table 9.1 shows the data as collected in part number sequence. These have been analysed to give issues value (annual turnover value), and then ranked in terms of this turnover value.

In Table 9.2, the data have been sorted into descending order of issue value. In this example all the items have usage, so there are no D-class items. The items have therefore been classified as A = 10 per cent, B = 20 per cent, C = 70 per cent.

The overall result of the analysis in this example is shown in Table 9.3. The focus on getting the A-class inventory correct becomes obvious from the summary. That is not to infer that the C-class items are not as imporant;

Table 9.1   Example of Pareto analysis

Item	Annual usage (units)	Unit cost (£)	Annual turnover (£)	Annual turnover (%)	Rank
A12	21	7	147	2.1	5
B23	105	11	1155	16.2	2
C34	2	15	30	0.4	10
D45	50	5	250	3.5	4
E56	9	14	126	1.8	6
F67	397	12	4764	66.8	1
G78	5	8	40	0.6	9
H89	500	1	500	7.0	3
I90	11	4	44	0.6	8
J01	3	25	75	1.1	7
Total			7131	100	

Table 9.2   Classification by usage value

Item	Annual usage (units)	Unit cost (£)	Annual turnover (£)	Annual turnover (%)	Rank	Class	Cumulative percentage
F67	397	12	4764	66.8	1	A	66.8
B23	105	11	1155	16.2	2	B	83.0
H89	500	1	500	7.0	3	B	90.0
D45	50	5	250	3.5	4	C	93.5
A12	21	7	147	2.1	5	C	95.6
E56	9	14	126	1.8	6	C	97.3
J01	3	25	75	1.1	7	C	98.4
I90	11	4	44	0.6	8	C	99.0
G78	5	8	40	0.6	9	C	99.6
C34	2	15	30	0.4	10	C	100.0
Total			7131	100			

Table 9.3   Summary of ABC analysis

Classification	Percentage of items*	Percentage of value	Value per class
A	10.0	66.8	4764
B	20.0	23.2	1655
C	70.0	10.0	712
Total	100.0	100	7131

*ABC analysis is carried out only for items with usage

however, a little inaccuracy can be covered by a touch of extra inventory, whereas for A-class items that would be too costly.

Having separated the items into A, B and C, the cycle counting can be organized.

Organizing the cycle count

Instead of having an annual wall-to-wall stocktake to count the number of items in the warehouse, it is preferable to carry out a routine assessment throughout the year instead. This cycle counting process has a number of advantages:

- it provides accurate stock records throughout the year
- a better quality of information is produced in stocktaking
- it costs less, since it can be carried out as part of the weekly store routines
- there is less disruption of work (no 'closed for stocktaking' days)
- it provides the opportunity to spend time to examine the causes of discrepancies.

Many stocktaking systems are based upon splitting the inventory into the four categories, A, B, C and D, according to their turnover value. The high turnover A-class items are counted frequently, and the D-class items (non-movers) are seldom counted. It is accepted by major auditing companies that D items do not have to be counted every year because of the relatively low turnover. Where there is a large number of items in this category, the total amount of stock checking is reduced.

> Don't do a wall-to-wall stocktake annually – it's disruptive and inaccurate.

For example, for a company with stocks of 1000 different items, the perpetual inventory system can be carried out according to the programme shown in Table 9.4.

Table 9.4   Example of the perpetual inventory system

Category	Frequency of stock checks	No. of items per 100 stock	No. of checks/ weeks
A	4-monthly	10	8
B	6-monthly	200	8
C	1-yearly	600	12
D*	3-yearly	100	1
Total			29

*The number of items in Class D depends on the number of non-movers

Obviously, the stocktaking of 29 items per week is only a minor task compared with the complete stocktake of 1000. The organization of perpetual inventory (PI) is simple. A selection of items from categories A, B, C and D are checked each week according to the pattern shown, and the total stock is worked through in strict rotation so that at the end of the period all the items have been counted. Control of the checking can be maintained through a complete list of parts or by a computer system. The checks should also be entered on the normal stock records.

On occasions when stock checks are carried out for other purposes (e.g. physical stockouts, negative recorded stock etc.), these adjustments can be incorporated into the stock-checking cycle – thus avoiding extra readings.

Normally the stock-check procedure is to measure the total amount of the item in the whole stores area. With random location systems for high volume items, this involves the checking of a number of areas throughout the stores. If one of the designated locations does not contain an item, then the physical stock record has to have the quantity deducted. Even if the item is simply misplaced, it should be deducted from the stock record until it has been found. This is done so that the records always agree with what is available to meet demand, otherwise at the time of a discrepancy it is uncertain whether the item is in the stores or not. Conversely, there may be an extra quantity of an item in a location not recorded.

The simple perpetual inventory system of checking part numbers requires a back-up to make sure that all inventory is counted. For this reason, the record system should also identify the locations that have been counted. This can be done by checking off against a location record for each count, and then inspecting the remaining locations each year to ensure that they are empty of certain items recorded subsequent to the check. Computer systems can also provide this information from the PI checking routine.

The perpetual inventory technique needs to be carried out rigorously, comparing physical checks with stock records and making adjustments where necessary. The stock records need to be up to date when the checks are made, and any items in dispatch or inspection areas have to be dealt with in a consistent manner or treated as separate storage areas with their own independent stock records. Unless the stores and records are maintained in a simple manner, much time is wasted in reconciling adjustments. The best method of operating is to close off the stores at regular weekly intervals, and carry out the check then.

Before the week's checking cycle begins, the following should be completed:

Receipts	All receipts booked	All goods put away
Dispatches	Dispatches deducted	All items put on transport or in locations, so the dispatch bay is empty
Supplier inventory	Treated separately	Kept in segregated area
Customer returns	Booked back in and treated separately	Located in quarantine stores
Identified errors	Errors from previous PI check corrected	Previous discrepancies re-checked

There is the temptation to use the PI checking time or manpower for urgent stores work, receiving or dispatching, but this must not be allowed. If there is insufficient control of stores personnel, then the PI checking should be carried out by individuals from another area, such as accounts.

Defining the requirements

If the inventory records are very inaccurate, or if there is open access to the store, then more effort has to be placed on the cycle counting process. For A-class items this may mean counting every four weeks (B-class items every two months, C-class items every four months) until the accuracy improves. Remember that there will only be a limited improvement by counting more frequently; the real way to reduce errors is root cause analysis – understand what the process is that allows the errors, and then change the process. The analysis of the problem is the key activity, not the counting.

> *Use the PI check to sort out why the records are going wrong.*

In order to start a new PI checking procedure, the following steps are required:

1. Assess the benefits from the cyclic inventory review and get agreement to proceed
2. Devise a perpetual inventory system that is appropriate for these areas to be counted
3. Identify the procedures that should be adopted by the inventory checkers and the disciplines required, and prepare an operating guide
4. Verify that the system is acceptable to accounts and auditors for the gradual phasing out of physical stocktakes
5. Pilot the cycle counting to make sure that the processes work in practice.

The introduction of PI checking enables the inventory to be checked at the slackest times, so labour efficiency can be increased. It has to be carried out to a plan without fail if it is to be the basis for audit valuation. As a result, the cycle counting method can be an accurate and effective way to improve inventory accuracy.

Summary

- Organize the stock into geometric patterns so that the quantity can be seen immediately.
- Use stacking, repetitive container size and layout to minimize errors.
- If an annual stocktake is essential, minimize the amount of writing and keying required.
- Review cycle counting and the procedures.
- Agree with the auditors that perpetual inventory checking can supersede an annual stock count.
- Devise a PI checking procedure that is practical and acceptable for valuation purposes.
- Focus the procedure on finding the basic causes of discrepancies and then putting them right.

10

Accuracy through information technology

- Getting the best accuracy from the computer systems
- Bar coding as an accuracy technique
- How to apply bar coding
- What to avoid when using bar coding
- Weigh counting
- Benefits from portable terminals
- Radio frequency tagging

Overview

There is usually a technological answer to a management problem. The development of computer-based records has enabled inventory across an enterprise to be linked, which avoids duplication of recording and provides visibility of the whole inventory balance (see Chapter 8). This is a powerful tool in improving accuracy, and new developments will continue to become available to make the maintenance of accurate records easier. Advances from simple automatic counting devices linked to computers through to item recognition technology are now available, and often at surprisingly little cost.

> *Take advantage of new technology.*

There are many stories of high expenditure and projects that fail. Care should therefore be taken to identify specifically what is to be achieved by new technology, and then to plan implementation in the way outlined in Chapter 11. Some of the key techniques are discussed in this chapter.

Stores computing

It is not necessary any longer to convince people that inventory computing is a good thing. The impact on record accuracy has major benefits, but these can be lost if it is used incorrectly. Benefits are maximized if the procedures enable the following:

- input of transactions into the computer without having them written out beforehand
- fast and simple updating of records
- computations by the computer, and not the inputter (e.g. number of items on several pallets, etc.)
- choice of data from a menu instead of inputting item codes or other information
- linked transactions between various stages and activities
- creation of management and control information without effort (e.g. negative stocks)
- automatic identification of exceptions and inaccuracies.

Computer software should contain checks and balances, and some logic to ensure that the data is within limits or has valid identity (for example, the system should check on the existence of the item code and that the quantity on the transaction is within the plausible range of quantities). In addition, the system can be used to create extra information for verification (e.g. descriptions) and control information, such as batch identity and record sequencing.

> *A good detailed inventory control system is the basis for accurate records.*

The system has to be capable of coping with the requirements of inventory recording in detail. The basic requirements for an inventory system, if there is to be the chance of accurate records, are:

- multilocation options on the stock record
- allocation options
- transfers between locations
- ABC classification
- real-time operation.

If paperwork can be avoided, then so will inaccuracies. In fact, paperwork is only required in the control process if signatures are needed, or if it is essential that information is required in locations away from terminals (for instance, as identity labels or picking lists).

Bar coding

Computers have a basic defect: they cannot read what they have written. The advent of effective character recognition by computers has been expected imminently for the last 30 years. The first method for producing information from the computer which it could then read was using Hollerith cards – punched cards, where the computer reads and interprets the sequence of holes. This technique was used with mechanical calculating devices and computers, and went out of fashion before alternatives were available.

It was not until bar coding became available that a universally acceptable alternative was found. These days bar codes are found on most consumer products, retail businesses being at the forefront of their use. They allow supermarkets to use individuals with limited numeracy skills on the check-outs, they can process a large number of transactions very fast, and stock control and management information is produced accurately, automatically and immediately. In fact, the reasons for using bar coding as a means of computer input are precisely these:

- accuracy
- speed of transactions.

Bar coding can be the complete solution to stock accuracy problems, because the input and output of data is so much more precise. This eliminates a large variety of causes of inaccuracy at a stroke. For those companies where the major sources of error are due to keying or identification, bar coding is an ideal tool.

The second advantage of bar coding – speed of transactions – enables an almost ideal situation to be reached, where stock records are immediately down-dated as the movement occurs. This means that the stock record really does equal the bin stock all the time, so anyone checking the quantity at any time can be confident in making corrections if there is a difference. This has major advantages when picking or checking (see Chapter 6).

The speed of transaction and the ease with which counting can be carried out allows stores personnel to apply finer control to the stock. If it is simple enough to do, then internal stores movements can be recorded:

- from goods receiving to locations
- from location to dispatch
- between locations of all sorts
- on loans and temporary issues
- on rejects awaiting decisions on scrap or rework
- on transactions not normally recorded.

Without bar coding, recording these movements can be too time consuming to be practical; it can only be carried out as long as the recording process is fast and simple to do. Bar coding can therefore add a new dimension to tracking and controlling items within stores and, of course, in all situations – including distributed inventory and in the process through a manufacturing plant.

Bar-coding options

There is a variety of ways to use bar codes, and the effectiveness of the application will depend on this choice. Bar codes provide a powerful tool in any inventory situation, and most easily when the stock is organized so that:

- items are supplied in small quantities or fixed pack sizes
- items are received and dispatched in the same pack sizes
- customers require items to have bar coding to match their own system
- items or packs are supplied with coding pre-printed specifically to meet the requirements.

It is easy to see that the simple swiping of a pack into stock and another swipe when it leaves stock is a simple process that is unlikely to lead to errors.

The improvement of accuracy through bar coding can ride on the back of a variety of other applications:

- stock control
- quality management
- traceability and lot tracking
- progress monitoring (e.g. in manufacturing)
- logistics (package tracking in transport and distribution).

In the process of improving the management of these processes through bar coding, the record accuracy also becomes better. Bar codes can be used to record:

- inventory identification
- inventory location
- quantity held
- destination or customer
- batch or serial number
- revision, release number or quality
- dates (purchase, use-by, manufacture or transfer dates).

All of the above benefit aspects of accuracy. Ideally, coding simplifies identi-fication, locations and quantity held, but complications may arise that require the inclusion of the other topics on the list. In theory, the more data the more control; however, in practice, the increase in complexity and the risk of inaccuracy makes it better to keep to the basics. The situation should be examined to identify the minimum amount of information required from the list above in order to meet the typical needs of the business. The least number of aspects should be included in the code. A second bar-code label can be applied to cover extra temporary attributes or other features (e.g. serial numbers).

> *Get the bar code to record the full information.*

The bar code should be suitable for use throughout the company and pro-vide correct information for all departments. A bar code for a pack of 50 of an item received into stores is useless once the pack has been opened and some of the items removed. Conversely, it is equally useless to unwrap a pack in order to swipe the item bar code 50 times. The correct option has to be considered for each company, and often for each stock line.

Again, the principle is to make the transaction fast and accurate, so any technique that causes significant extra work should be considered as wrong. The starting point is therefore to take the recording procedure that is used manually and then consider how it can be modified to make it more useful, given the advantages which bar coding offers.

It is not essential for the bar code to be the same as the item identity code. This concept can be of use where there is no label printer and items without bar codes arrive at an area, or where items are already bar coded by the supplier. The essential requirement in this situation is that the computer can translate uniquely between the code arriving and the company's iden-tity code. The bar code, whatever it is, can be read into the computer and matched up with the item identity with which it is known in the company. Each time the label is read subsequently, the computer can look up the reference and translate to the appropriate code number.

> *Mirror or improve the current practice with the bar code.*

To record items without bar codes, all that is required is a series of sequential bar-code labels which are applied to the item as it is received. A reference table can then be created, which translates between the bar code and the item identity number.

What to bar code

The use of code readers should be a short cut – an advantage for the user. It should enable the user to do things more efficiently. The entry of data into the computer system is normally a mixture of bar coding and keying in; the keying in is more prone to inaccuracy, and therefore should be restricted to a minimum.

A common misconception is that all items have to be bar coded to start with. This is not true, although the more items that are bar coded, the greater the benefits. A starting point for using bar codes is to copy what is currently already bar coded when it arrives. The bar code can contain all the information for physical stock control – i.e. all the attributes listed above.

Taking the principle that the bar code should be useful throughout the whole of the company, the data can be considered as either fixed or variable. The fixed information should be on the item (or its packaging) as a bar code, while the variable information should be separate. This can also be as a bar code at a particular location, or kept as an easy-to-use record. For example, a box of 50 items passing through an inspection may have three bar codes used in the process: the item identity label that travels with the pack; a process traveller (a card that identifies that the item requires inspection, and that can be swiped when the item arrives and departs from the inspection area); and a 'cause of reject' card, which has a different bar code for each cause of failure.

In manufacturing, many companies use bar coding to identify the manufacturing batch of the product. This may be useful, but often only for traceability purposes – thus missing the potential for improving inventory accuracy.

> Use bar codes for labels, travellers and lists.

Bar-coding systems

There are several bar-code 'languages' available, some being numerical and others including letters as well. They are often industry standards, and the appropriate one should be chosen to match with those of customers or suppliers. In many situations bar-code readers will automatically identify which code is being used and read it at the same time.

Cost

Bar coding can be very cheap or very expensive, depending on the size, quality and sophistication of the system. The investment is normally well worthwhile because of the improvement in accuracy, but the improvement has to be costed. Costs can vary from a few hundred pounds for a single bar coder and software to hundreds of thousands for a full installation with communications and high-power remote readers.

> *Use bar codes as a cheap and effective way for speedy and accurate recording.*

Pitfalls in using bar codes

No solution to stock accuracy is infallible, and it is the input of information to the bar-coding system that gives potential for errors. These arise mainly through:

- creating the bar codes (the wrong code may be produced, or the label put onto the wrong item)
- reading the bar code (double swiping may occur, codes be illegible, or the wrong item read)
- mistiming of the read-out
- system faults.

Wrong code produced

Stand-alone bar-coding systems require data input to trigger the label production, which may result in the usual problems of keying and transcription errors. Bar-coding systems should therefore be linked to stock control and item movement systems, and the label creation process should also be linked to this. If systems are not yet linked, a newly produced label can be scanned immediately and the bar code checked against the data source.

Label put onto the wrong item

This can be avoided by good physical organization and layout. Each item to be labelled should be segregated and clearly identifiable. Only one type of item should be labelled at a time, and the labels should be produced as they are required in the same location as they are being applied. They should be applied to the goods immediately. If the item already has a label, this number should be visually the same as the figures on the bar-code label, and the two should be placed adjacently on the item for direct comparison. (For the sequential numbered labels described earlier in this chapter this comparison is not possible, so more care has to be taken to ensure that the bar code refers to the right item.)

Double swiping

Swiping the item twice can be a problem. Audible beeps for each swipe can warn the operative, and a display of the last transaction can help. Where single transaction types are the norm, the system can be made to inhibit repeat input. If this is suspected as a problem, the system can be organized such that repeat entries require a 'confirm' (i.e. enter) key as well.

Illegible codes

In some environments labels become damaged by water, dirt, oil etc., and it is important to ensure that the material of the label can withstand the situation in which it is likely to exist. Codes can normally be read through clear plastic, which helps in many situations. Although putting the code on the item or container of items is the ideal, there is always the alternative of putting the code onto the paperwork that moves with the item or is provided for that process.

If the item is large, then it is always useful to put bar-code labels on different parts of it (this is particularly useful for palletized goods).

> Devise the procedures carefully so they cannot lead to confusion or mistakes.

Wrong item read

Reading the wrong label can be avoided by good housekeeping. There should be separate locations, when picking or at a dispatch bay, for checked and unchecked items. A routine to follow will limit mistakes.

Care has to be taken, especially when stock checking *in situ*. If the location has a bar code and the item has a separate one, then any duplication can be analysed out when auditing the transactions.

Mistiming of read-out

Timing has been discussed as a key problem with record accuracy, and bar coding has the potential for immediate update of the system. If hand-held bar coders are used, they are either interactive with the main system or downloaded when the set of transactions is completed (which may be hours later). This lag between the transaction and downloading to the stock control system can be a major constraint on maintaining accuracy. First of all, there should be no stock checking during this interval. Then the procedures should be modified to return the bar coder to the download at frequent intervals.

System faults

During the implementation of bar-code systems there is the potential for system error, but this should be minimized as long as a standard package is used. Fortunately bar-code hardware is usually a 'plug & play' installation, so the bar-code readers are up and running very easily.

Weak areas of the system include the interface between the bar-coding system and the inventory recording system. The robustness of the data collection process should also be checked during implementation. What happens if the system or power fails during transfer? What back-up is there for retrieving data as a result of problems with the readers or software? How good are the bar coders at reading under the typical stores operating conditions?

Weigh counting

Weigh counting in between processes and for movements in and out of stores is a very good method for counting many types of items. The banks use this for counting money, so it can obviously be quite accurate. Sample scales are the best, where the weight of a small sample of the items (a dozen or two) is used to calibrate the scale so that the number of items in the whole batch can be calculated. The normal weigh counter will read out the number of items rather than the weight of the bulk. The weigh counter can, of course, produce a bar-code label, which can then be attached to the items – thus avoiding subsequent transcription errors.

Weigh counting should be carried out carefully to ensure that accuracy is maintained. The weight of the container must be allowed for by deducting a fixed allowance or the actual weight from the gross recording. It is just as important to have the correct weight of the container as it is for the items, so the same accuracy of measurement should be used for this.

Sometimes individuals want to overestimate the quantity. There are many situations where this may occur – suppliers trying to charge for more than they deliver, production workers wanting a bonus for making extra, sales personnel enhancing the sales figures etc. Care should be taken to see that foreign pieces of materials, soil or dirt are not present in the container, and that items are not wet or covered with material that will increase their weight significantly.

There were several tricks traditionally used by old-fashioned scrap dealers, who would bring in their wagons wet, or with extra spare wheels, in order to maximize the incoming weight over a weighbridge. The excess weight was then discarded before leaving the yard so that the outgoing fully-loaded wagon weight was reduced and they only had to pay for the minimum amount of scrap.

Electronic scales can be linked up to the computer system to provide a direct input of the quantity of items. The item number or description, or transaction type, has to be recorded at the same time using other means or codes.

Weighing is a convenient method of counting inventory, but it has to be incorporated in the existing processes of the business, otherwise it will cause extra work and delays.

Monitoring manufacturing work in progress by automatic recording devices

For businesses where there is a continuous flow of goods, as in packaging or manufacturing, in-line counters are the obvious answer. Ideally, in manufacturing, machinery can be fitted with counting devices that detect one of the following:

1. The number of operations (e.g. strokes, insertions, cuts etc.) done by the equipment
2. The number of products produced in the equipment
3. The number of good products produced.

These are three stages of sophistication, which give three levels of accuracy. A machine counter of the first type is the simplest to set up, but does suffer from inaccuracies caused by:

- running equipment for set-up
- test quantities not used afterwards
- substandard production at start-up
- out-of-specification products
- running equipment during cleaning/maintenance.

The major causes of over-counting are normally the use of equipment during the setting up of a job where the optimism of supervision or operator, or the nuisance of setting the recorder causes extra operations to be recorded.

This is avoided by using the second type of detector, typically monitored by a product sensor on the output from the equipment. This again can give inflated readings, because it counts poor quality output as well as good quality product. Scrap recording, can, of course, supplement this and create good accurate records, but is not recommended as a reliable method.

> Counting devices situated between processes can give precise measurement of the numbers passing.

The best method is therefore by using the third type of detector, where the product is automatically checked for critical facets of quality as it is produced. The checking may be anything from a simple operator test (for example, checking an item on a test rig as part of a production process) to an automated statistical process control (SPC) system that modifies the settings on a process to maintain quality production, and rejects faulty work should it ever happen. This not only ensures a high degree of counting accuracy for inventory recording systems, but also gives major benefits in quality through:

- direct recording and statistical variance analysis to avoid out-of-specification output
- the mechanism to close off production of out-of-specification products are produced
- feedback of information directly to the production equipment to adjust conditions to ensure that the product is always made within specification.

Normally, the cost saving in improved performance or elimination of scrap from this feedback control loop quickly justifies the cost of the more sophisticated approach. Record accuracy benefits will enhance the benefits from direct quality monitoring on equipment, and help to justify the capital cost of it.

As with other technical improvements, the linking of this equipment into the inventory system enhances inventory recording accuracy.

The same approach can obviously be taken for fluids, where the flow-rate meters are an integral part of the inventory monitoring system. The challenge here is often to ensure that the tolerances on the measurements are small enough to enable accurate cumulative inventory measurement.

Portable terminals

To achieve the basic requirement of accuracy, the record has to be down-dated at the same time as the physical process is carried out (receipt, picking, dispatch etc.). Any other approach leads to complexity and inaccuracy. The development over the years of small, convenient PCs, workstations and palm-held terminals now provides the technology through which this can be achieved. Instantaneous recording can be achieved using these mobile terminals at the time the transaction is made. The mobile terminal enables stores operatives effectively to carry around the full stock records with them, giving the full control that this implies.

Linking this record to the rest of the business through a radio communications link provides a second and additional major benefit. A radio link to the computer network enables records to be maintained correctly. As the whole company can now have this up-to-the-minute information, there is an additional dimension – credibility.

> *Operators with all the information at their fingertips can be much more effective at maintaining accuracy and responding to business needs.*

The use of mobile terminals gives other advantages:

- stock balances can be checked with confidence while picking, knowing that the records are up-to-date
- alternative locations and lines can be located immediately
- priority orders can be included in the picking sequence as they are received
- corrections and queries can be logged directly into the system as they are discovered
- low stocks and shortages can be noted from the physical stock immediately
- immediate information can be provided to all system users (sales, quality, technical etc.)
- no paperwork processing and filing is needed after the transaction
- automatic analysis and valuation of stock is done without any extra work.

Summary of current technological solutions

It is clear that inaccurate records can be avoided through the use of technical solutions. However, those wanting to improve accuracy should not rely upon information technology for answers. Major improvements will be achieved through better control and procedures before there is the need to spend significant amounts on technology. It is usually much faster to make operational changes than to justify, purchase and implement technical solutions.

The cumulative effect of computer-based solutions enables a much higher level of accuracy to be achieved. The basic techniques of bar coding, portable terminals and communication links with terminals form the platform on which modern stores records, and movements outside stores, can be maintained easily and accurately. Stores personnel in future may be surprised to find that record accuracy was ever a problem, since they will have the basic automatic recording technology to ensure that they have very few problems.

Radio frequency identification

Another technique that is available and even more powerful than bar coding is the automatic identification of an item using a radio frequency tag (radio frequency identification, or RFID). It is not harmful or costly, and nor does it require any effort for recording.

The essence of this technique is to have a loop of wire included in the label on the goods (the wire can be built into the fabric, so it is not obtrusive or bulky). When this passes though a detector (often a wire running round the stores door), the frequency characteristic of the loop resonates and the signal is translated into the correct code. Hence it automatically updates the computer with a transaction.

This presents the prospect of stock issues being recorded automatically when the items are removed from the stores, even if the person does not do anything to get them recorded – and even if someone makes an informal issue when the stores area is not manned. This could be a major advantage where items are required on a 24-hour basis, but where it is not worth stores being manned at all hours.

> *Automatic recording of movements through RFID saves a lot of missed issues.*

The technology is not new, having been developed in the 1940s for the differentiation between friendly and enemy aircraft. The systems can be robust if organized properly. The reason for the limited use of RFID probably owes more to ignorance that it exists and is usable, than to the quality of the method. The technique has taken a long time to find significant application, but now that inventory accuracy is becoming much more of a major issue it could well become much more widespread. Obviously there are some special situations where the goods themselves may interfere with the technique, but this is not a significant problem.

Summary

- Technology can make it easy to keep accurate records.
- Make the store a centre for IT excellence.
- Everyone should be using bar coding for recording.
- Bar coding can be a cheap solution.
- Make the use of bar codes very simple and avoid the usual pitfalls.
- Use the available technology – weigh counting, portable computing, and self identification for items.

11

Record accuracy as a project

- Why have accurate records?
- The approach to improving accuracy
- The role of executive teams and project teams
- Planning the process
- Ensuring that there is progress

Project teams

Record inaccuracy causes much nuisance, but most people will avoid tackling it, assuming it is a failure on someone else's part. After all, it's just caused by people not counting properly or doing the paperwork correctly. The lack of appeal of solving the inaccuracy may be because it requires practical application, a great deal of detailed work and no guarantee of success. This is why record accuracy should be approached as a project. It can provide the impetus for major improvements over a short length of time, which can then be maintained at the new level through improved disciplines and company operations after the project. The approach as a development project enables the focus to be put on accuracy and the application of additional resources to get it right. The project needs the normal ingredients of a development project:

- Objectives
- Project teams
- Resources
- Commitment to change.

Improve accuracy through concerted, focused projects.

Objectives

The objectives take the form of an agreed increase in record accuracy in a specific area over a fixed timescale. The targets should be quantitative, and generally agreed amongst those involved in inventory control and in the project. When the business is reviewing inventory recording, it may be a good time to look at the method of measuring accuracy and the tolerances previously set.

Project teams

The investigation of accuracy will take many directions, and so the workload must be spread amongst as many people as practicable. It is useful to have a two-layer structure in the project, comprising an executive team and a series of focused action teams.

The executive team is there to hold the programme together and to act as a coordination centre for the action teams. It consists of senior members of management who have an interest in the results of better record accuracy. They are there to guide the overall direction of the projects, and to add weight to the focus on the project. They will also have the power to allocate manpower, funds and outside resources to the improvement projects. The team can perform its function by holding meetings, typically every six weeks, at which the action teams report progress and identify further targets. Direct involvement in action teams is not an essential function for the executives, as long as they provide active backing.

The action teams consist of a few (perhaps three) individuals who are knowledgeable about an area that is considered to be a cause of inaccuracy. They should have closely defined objectives, and should only veer from these as a result of discussion with the executive team. Their role is to investigate a specific perceived problem with a view to implementing changes that give improvements. It is often easier to identify external causes of a problem, and thus be unable to make improvements. The teams therefore have to focus on what they can achieve within their terms of reference, and allow other teams to work on other causes.

Resources

One of the reasons for inaction is the lack of time to do anything. For improvements to be made, people have to be committed to working on the project over a short period. Once action teams have been allocated, the success will depend on their ability and any external support – people, material, or capital expenditure needed. Reporting back to the executive team is a direct by-product of their work. As the individuals undoubtedly have other direct work to do, the projects must be fitted in around their workload. It is important to ensure at the outset that participants realistically estimate and agree their true availability for the project.

Commitment to change

The members of the action teams are ideally volunteers who think that it is possible to make a difference. Many people believe that they are in a powerless position and cannot make changes, and do not believe that the role of management has changed from 'directing' to 'facilitating' in their own business. The individuals in the team need to believe that change is beneficial – for themselves and for the business.

> *Two types of teams are needed – a top management team to provide resources and commitment, and action teams to make changes.*

Setting up the project

The first step in setting up the project is to bring together the executive team, who can identify the overall objectives of and possible participants in the project. Since record accuracy is often taken as an insurmountable problem, it is useful for the participants to have their awareness raised about the costs of inaccuracy and the potential methods (described in this book!) that exist for improving accuracy. A formal lecture can provide some good ideas, and at the same time raise awareness and encourage the commitment to make changes.

A good way to start the actual project is to have a brainstorming session on the causes of record inaccuracy. This is normally integral with the theory session. The brainstorming session will provide a list of possible causes of inaccuracy, with suggestions regarding which are likely to be important and which less so. Action teams can then be created as a result of this session. Each action team should take one of the causes that is considered more troublesome and set out to investigate and cure it, developing work schedules and milestones and agreeing these with the executive team. Action teams that are not making progress should be disbanded. If there is a record accuracy issue still to be solved, a new team should be set up with modified terms of reference, or a team that will approach the situation differently.

At the conclusion of each action project, the changes that are being implemented have to be presented by the project team as a new company process to ensure that the change will not revert to the previous situation.

Steps for improving record accuracy

The process for improving accuracy really starts by convincing people that:

- records are unacceptably poor
- it is possible to improve them
- there is a benefit to the teams and a significant business benefit in the project.

Once this resistance to change has been overcome in a nucleus of people, project teams can be arranged, both at executive and operational level. Once real commitment has been made at the top of the company, the process for improvement can commence. The steps normally used for each project team are:

1. Brainstorming
2. Analysis
3. Action planning
4. Monitoring
5. Reporting.

Brainstorming

The first process is to suggest as many ideas as possible as to what is creating the problems identified for the team. The ideas arising in the brainstorming sessions can be sensible, far-fetched, frivolous, stupid – any form of suggestion is acceptable during brainstorming. One idea builds upon another.

Analysis

The work of brainstorming has to be analysed to give types of ideas, which are assessed for their likelihood and importance. Which of these factors are likely to lead to errors? The analysis is a difficult job, because it needs both an understanding of the issues and an open mind in order to get the best out of the more extreme suggestions. Some of the most outrageous ideas can lead to the best benefits. The result of the analysis will be a priority list of areas to investigate.

Action planning

The action teams have to work out a priority sequence for tackling the inaccuracies. They have to define a plan of action and how the tasks can be accomplished, given the limitations expected on manpower and other resources.

> *Start with the easier but significant problems.*

An outline plan for an action team could answer the following sequence of questions:

- What are the detailed objectives?
- What are the major steps required?
- What method of approach should be used?
- Who will be involved in planning and actions?
- What are the tasks to be done, and how long will they take?
- How is the success of the project to be judged?
- When can results begin to be seen, and what is the total timescale?

Projects are most successful when they are well planned, so the identification of people, tasks and timescales should be carried out at the outset, knowing that the tasks are likely to change as the project progresses. The project plan should identify milestones – tasks completed at specified times through which progress can be judged. The use of simple planning charts and critical path analysis can ensure that a project is controlled properly, and helps to maintain the timescales.

Monitoring

It is important that a project team works as a cohesive unit, carrying out the various tasks and then discussing the results. The initial approach to the objectives will almost certainly have to be revised in the light of the results that team members report. It is very important to make time for discussion and development of ideas within the team if the real causes of record inaccuracy are to be tracked down. If the project takes place over several weeks, it is useful to keep some notes from these discussions to track the development and also to assist in reporting to the executive team. The use of graphical display boards should be encouraged to identify issues and progress, since they give an immediate visual impact to everyone working in the business.

> *Don't let the timescales slip because of delayed meetings.*

Reporting

Feedback to the executive team on a regular basis is most important. It ensures the involvement of senior executives who can clear the way for further actions by the teams, sanction expenditure and communicate success. The reporting process also enables the project teams to take stock of progress and renew their plans.

The action teams' reports include:

- progress against the action objectives and project milestones passed
- major issues and constraints on progress
- support required from outside the action team
- revised targets and benefits from the project.

The executive team has to take their role in running projects very seriously:

- meetings should be held at regular (monthly) intervals, with full participation of the executive team
- full support should be given to the action teams, with resources and budgets if necessary
- commitment to achieving the end result should be demonstrated
- communication of successes to other parts of the business is also very useful; this will change the attitude toward records and make other people consider their actions that contribute to inaccuracies.

By following these normal and simple planning processes, significant improvements can be made in record accuracy. The emphasis is then on consolidating the changes and making it impossible to slip back to the former ways.

Summary

- Improve accuracy through a concentrated effort of project teams.
- There needs to be commitment and involvement from the top.
- Carry out a series of small specific projects on the major areas of concern.
- Have formal and open progress meetings at key stages.
- Focus on aspects that can be implemented by the participants.
- Start with some easier options to give the projects momentum.

12

The management of record accuracy

> - Steps in improving accuracy
> - How to achieve success

Monitoring accuracy

The methods by which accuracy can be measured have already been discussed in Chapter 1. The two aspects – tolerance and success rate – have to be balanced to give the right focus for improvement. Record accuracy should be one of the routine management control statistics reported at management meetings – routine in the sense that it is always reported, and not in the sense that is passed over in the reports.

Once the structure of setting up the executive team and action teams has been organized, the process for reviewing and managing the project is as follows:

1. Decide on the measure of accuracy to be used
2. Set up a monitoring routine
3. Designate the people involved and their procedures
4. Use a simple tabular or graphical presentation of the weekly/monthly information
5. Set targets and milestones for improvement during projects
6. When milestones are reached, review the accuracy as projects proceed and carry out corrective action where necessary
7. Tighten up the monitoring targets as accuracy improves.

Setting the targets is a matter of compromise between what is required and what is practical. When setting accuracy targets, we should bear in mind the importance of the area in terms of stock value, the effect of inaccuracy and the practicality of achieving an improvement. The prime objective is to achieve acceptable accuracy (i.e. accuracy that does not impair business performance significantly).

Setting practical, achievable targets is essential if they are going to be acceptable to the people concerned. A series of small steps is better than trying to solve the whole problem at once. Setting out to improve one area at a time will enable people to focus on improvements in that area. By commencing in an easy area and improving the situation an environment of success is created, which can then be used to aid performance in other areas.

Making it happen

Inventory accuracy has been discussed in some detail in this book. Many potential causes of inaccuracy have been suggested, and ways of improving it have been examined. The current level of discrepancies that you may be experiencing probably arise from a combination of the causes. As most of the errors arise from just two or three causes, the first step is to get some evidence for what these are likely to be – not an easy task. Analysis is often difficult. (Failing good analysis, it is always possible to guess – elimination of the chief suspect may not in the end improve accuracy, but it is one potential problem solved.)

By following the ideas in this book, record accuracy can be improved. You are now in a good position to decide what steps can be taken to reduce the level of inaccuracy in your own company. What is now required is a list of actions that you consider should be taken to improve the situation, followed by project management.

When it comes down to it, all we are trying to do is to count how many there are. It shouldn't be too difficult if those involved have:

- the motivation
- the authority
- the need

and, of course, the backing from their bosses.

Summary

- Now that you have come to the end of this book, it's up to you to do something.
- All these techniques have been tried and tested; choose the right combination and success is assured.
- Ensure that your reading time and the author's time have not been wasted!

Appendix 1

Formula for generating stores location check digits

The check digits for confirming that stock is put away in the correct location can be generated simply on a spreadsheet. The logic for allocating numbers ensures that each location has a different code, and the computer can create the code from the location number. (Check digits are discussed in Chapter 5.)

A location code often consists of four digits, with the following form: two numbers followed by one letter followed by one number, corresponding to aisle location followed by rack position followed by shelf height number.

An identity code is worked out from the four digits using the formula:

Identity code: $+2600 * \text{CODE}(\text{LEFT}(\text{location},1)) + 260 * \text{CODE}(\text{MID}(\text{location},2,1)) + 10 * \text{CODE}(\text{MID}(E2,3,1)) + 1 * \text{CODE}(\text{RIGHT}(\text{location},1))$

This is shown in Table A.1.

This identity code is then converted to a digit using the formula:

Check digit $= \text{CHAR}(+\text{identity code}-138252-\text{INT}((\text{identity code}-138252)/65) * 65 + 51)$

The identity code is put on the location and keyed back in to confirm that the item has been located properly.

Table A.1   Location check digits

Location	Check digit	Code
00a0	a	138298
00b0	k	138308
00b9	3	138317
01a1	b	138559
01a2	c	138560
01a3	d	138561
01a4	e	138562
01a9	j	138567
01b0	k	138568
01b9	3	138577
03a2	c	139080
05a3	d	139601
09z5	\	140893
10a1	b	140899
10a2	c	140900
10z5	\	141153
11a0	a	141158
11a1	b	141159
11a2	c	141160

Index

ABC analysis, 101–3
Action planning, 125
Annual stocktaking, 96
Arrays, 95–6
Audit, operations, 68
    balance, 69
Automatic recording devices, 117–21

Backflushing, 86–8
Bar coding, 110–16
    options, 111
    pitfalls, 114–16
Batch control, 75–83
    identification, 75
    progress control, 77–83
    quantities, 75–7
Batching, 95
Benefits from accurate records, 16–24
Brainstorming, 125

Cando, 41
Check digit systems, 59–60, 130–1
Colour coding, 40
Consignment stocks, 44
Control areas, 64
Coordinated batches, 63
Cost of inaccuracy, 17–21

Counting methods, 93–6
    direct, 94
    weigh, 94, 116–17
Cycle counting, 100–1
    organization of, 104

Dispatch control, 68

Effects of record accuracy, 16–17
Enclaves of stock, 50
Enclosed stores, 66
Excess inventory, 21–3
External storage, 44

Failsafing (*Pokeyoka*), 39, 61–2
Financial control of stock value, 92
Flow of material, 63
Formula for check digits, 130
Foundations of accurate records, 46–8

Goods inward, 68

Improving record accuracy, 125
Inaccuracy, 25–35
    analysis of underlying reasons, 28–35
    causes of, 28
    observations of, 25–7

Information control, 34–5
Information quality, 48–9
Information technology, 108–21
Input/output monitoring, 88–90
Inventory checking, 93–107
    low levels, 36–7
    vendor managed, *see* VMI
    zero, 37
Item identity, 57–9

Just-in-time, 36

Kanban, 41
Kit marshalling, 84–6

Layout of stores, 69–71
Lean stock levels, 36
Level of accuracy, 5
Locked stores, 52–4

Management of record accuracy,
    128–9
Material balance, 90–2
Measuring accuracy, 8–11
Monitoring, 126, 128–9
Monitoring WIP, 117–18
Motivation, 55
MRP, 17

Objectives of accurate records, 6
Operations audit, 68
Ownership of stock, 49–52

Paperwork, 30–2, 97
Pareto curve, 101–2
People factor, 54
Perpetual inventory system, 104–6
Physical inventory checking, 67
Portable terminals, 118–19

Project–record accuracy, 122–4
    resources, 122
    setting up, 124
    teams, 122

Quantity counters, 95

Radio frequency identification
    (RFID), 120
Real time recording, 71–4
Reasons for having accurate records, 4
Record pro formas, 14–15
Recording system, 55–7
Reducing stock, 37
Reporting, 127
Responsibilities for accuracy, 46–60

Security, 65
Shortages, 23–4
Simplification, 38
SKU, 44
Stacking, 96
Stock movement, 84–92
Stocktaking, 96–100
    procedures, 99
    systems, 98
Stores computing, 108
Structures to avoid inaccuracy, 36–45
Supply chain, 61

Targets of accuracy, 11–14
Tolerances, 12–15

Unwanted transfers, 49

VMI, 36, 42

Weigh counting, 94, 116–17

Zero inventory, 37